Praise for Michael Pritchard

Pritchard is a kind and funny man who wants to prevent the unaddressed grief of children from turning to anger, rage, and violence as they grow older... What really sets him apart is the humanity and authenticity of his material...

Wall Street Journal

[Michael Pritchard's] commitment and dedication as our opening keynote speaker proved to be instrumental to the overwhelming success of the conference!
National Youth Crime Prevention Council - Washington DC

The best keynote presenter we've ever had.

Dept. of Social Services NY

Michael Pritchard received a Doctorate of Humane Letters from Hartwick University for a lifetime of work inspiring and motivating hundreds of thousands of children and parents across the nation.

Copyright © 2005 Michael Pritchard

ISBN 1-4116-2246-4

Published by Heartland Media, California, USA.

PRINTED IN THE UNITED STATES OF AMERICA

Cover art and design by Dan Spencer

Listen To What Your Kids Aren't Telling You

Michael Pritchard

with Dan Spencer

Preface

"No one has yet realized the wealth of sympathy,
the kindness and generosity hidden in the soul of a child.
The effort of every true education should be
to unlock that treasure."
-Emma Goldman

No matter where I've traveled in North America – whether in the flatlands of Iowa, the streets of Mexico, the whaling villages of Alaska, the sidewalks of Brooklyn, the Canadian wilderness, or the posh California suburbs – I've met children with amazing stories to tell. Listening to kids express their pain and joy is incredibly enlightening, and I've been doing just that for over 25 years. This book is a compendium of some of the wonderful stories I heard and the important truths I discovered – truths that every adult should learn and understand.

The most profound discovery is that parents, more than anyone, need to rediscover the simple, classic art of listening to their kids. Every parent has experienced the following conversation.

Parent: How was school today?

Child: Good.

Parent: What happened?

Child: Nothing.

Parent: Did you have a good day?

Child: Yeah.

Most parents don't ask much more than that because they know how fruitless further prying can be. Digging for any more information beyond a few monosyllabic, mumbled grunts sometimes leads to anger and resentment or argumentation. But parents need to persevere. Be patient and draw out answers from your kids. Every parent wants to know what's going on in their children's heads and what experiences are shaping their personalities. Most parents realize there are truths that their kids aren't telling them. Not knowing can be frustrating. The only way to excavate those private truths is to be patient with your kids and truly listen. When a child screams or acts out or challenges us, we should listen past what they're saying and hear what it is they really need. In other words, aside from listening to what are kids *are* telling us, we also need to discover what kids *aren't* telling us.

Giving a child a forum to express himself or herself is empowering. Parents need to allow their kids to express their emotions. Unfortunately, for too many fathers and mothers it's an inconvenience to hear about their child's anxieties. Some parents try to diminish their children's problems as unimportant. These kids become marginalized so that they're barely in their parents' lives. That negates or minimizes the child's emotions, which can affect him or her in various ways. What parents need to understand is that kids can't learn and struggle for achievement in school and become who they need to become in a meaningful way until one's emotions are in balance with the brain. Only then can a student achieve what he or she needs to accomplish.

Having emotional balance is what it's all about, and too often parents have no concept of how deep their kids' feelings run. Teenagers are summarily dismissed with phrases like, "Oh, you're just growing up," or "It's a phase you're going through." This shows that parents aren't listening.

Some kids, of course, simply don't talk to their parents. But that doesn't mean you shouldn't draw them out of their shells. I have a son who is rather private. Some people may mistake this for shyness. Once, as a means of drawing out his feelings, he and I drove for several hours from our home to Sacramento and back. Just him and I. Very little was said the entire trip. But just as I pulled the car into our driveway – after the complete round trip – that was when my son finally opened up and said what he needed to say about his situation in life and his emotions. Privately, it struck me as pretty funny that we had been alone together for four hours yet he waited until the last moment to spill his guts to me. With a private person all it takes is to be with somebody and he or she will open up – when you go fishing together, when you sit on a public bench, when you hike or camp together.

Speakers at funerals sometimes discuss life reviewing. It's the opportunity to reflect on and realize regrets, like not finding the time to comprehend a child's emotions. But we can't afford to wait. Do it now. Be emotionally present with and conscious of your kids. Slow down and let your soul catch up to you. Be with them. Feel their pain. Hear them. Don't miss the opportunities to sit and be fully present with your child – to understand their feelings, to be conscious of their emotions – because we attain wisdom from it. That sharing of emotions is when we truly gather consciousness.

Parents must train themselves to be open to their kids' emotions. Be patient. Take time to be with your child. Wait for them to open up to you. If you show patience, they will bloom. As the Apaches say, in the stillness lies the answer.

Sadly, too many children in this world are the victims of verbal abuse. And much too often I hear about kids who try their best to please their parents only to discover that whatever they do is never good enough. No matter what faults we have as parents – drug abuse, alcohol abuse, anger from our own past – we need to understand that our children want nothing more than for us to care about them. To be a part of their lives. To enjoy them. To listen to them.

Ask your children about that other major factor in their lives besides family: school. Many kids feel anxiety because of tormenting, teasing, derision, ridicule, and humiliation by fellow students. School provides few outlets for expressing those feelings. Kids become more concerned about their own emotional survival than about what they can memorize for a math test.

As a result, educators are dealing with kids who are, for all intents and purposes, emotional tornados. Many of their students are spiritually depleted. If they understood the psychological distress of the boys and girls they teach, they'd have the same sympathy as if the kids were handicapped. Many children are, in fact, in emotional wheelchairs.

In order to teach children, you have to be able to hear their pain. If you're not willing to do that, you don't belong in modern education. You belong in that systematic 1950s paradigm in which the Baby Boomer generation grew up. Controlling students just to make them memorize material isn't effectual in the new millennium. Kids have issues that need to be addressed before they can be effectively taught. A young man will have a hard time remembering the year that Columbus set foot in the new world after his step-father punches him so hard in the back of the head that he needs stitches. A girl who is mocked and laughed at when her alcoholic mother comes to school in curlers and grungy clothes will have difficulty focusing on algebra. Although the traditional three Rs of education – reading, writing, and 'rithmatic – are as vital and valuable to students today as they ever were, kids in the 21st century need to be taught so much more. Our education system leans heavily on the worthy, stalwart lessons that feed the intellect, but our educators rarely teach the lessons that feed the heart and soul. Our kids also need the components that build character and emotional balance. We need to highlight the three additional Rs of learning: right, wrong, and real. We can't offer a 'well-rounded' education by omitting them.

Does that mean that all educators need to be psychiatrists, priests, rabbis, imams, or social workers? No. But teachers should help their students be more than just survivors and test takers. They need to instill in kids the ability to overcome personal dilemmas and to give those kids a sounding board for their troubles.

And one of the biggest problems they face is dealing with peers. Getting kids to speak out about what's bothering them and confronting one another teaches them that giving voice to their feelings is liberating. The truest sense of freedom for kids is to stand up before their peers and speak their minds, especially knowing that their tormentors may be among the group they're addressing. Children can take comfort knowing that most of their fellow students and friends want to do the right thing. I often ask kids, "How many of you want to attend a school where people are kind and compassionate and caring?" The responses are always overwhelmingly in favor.

This book provides stunning examples of kids who were permitted to freely express their feelings. The truths they told me run the gamut of emotions. Few people, whether parents or teachers or other caregivers, ever provided them the opportunity to speak out. I did, and the results often altered their young lives in positive ways.

I hope you'll see from reading these tales how important it is to get kids to open up and express their feelings and opinions, and how vital it is to pay attention. We can all learn a lot from listening to kids.

- Michael Pritchard

In the Beginning, There Were Parents

"When I was a boy of fourteen,
my father was so ignorant
I could hardly stand to have the old man around.
But when I got to be twenty-one,
I was astonished at how much he had learned."
- Mark Twain

I was so completely the opposite of my father. He was an Army drill instructor with one of those four-dollar haircuts; a dollar for each corner. He used to shine his shoes every night until he could see his reflection in them. His clothing drawers looked like a department store; everything was folded precisely. His bed sheets were systematically tucked in with expert precision. The lawn was mowed in perfect rows. By contrast, I was the biggest pig known to mankind. I wore the same socks for weeks. I'd do anything to get out of chores. I preferred a beating to cleaning my room and mowed the lawn in exotic patterns while I chased the dog with the lawnmower. I was the ultimate smart aleck.

When I was a boy, my Dad used to take the entire family for Sunday drives. One afternoon, I was in the back seat of our car tormenting my three older brothers. Finally, my Father couldn't take it anymore. He screeched the car to a stop on the side of the road, and with that drill instructor voice turned and pointed at me in the back seat.

"Remind me to kill you when we get home!"

My brothers and I would sit frozen and biting our lips because we were scared to death. But we quietly continued taunting and trying to make each other laugh just to get in trouble. As soon as Dad pulled the car into the driveway, I had to say it.

"Hey, Dad, you told me to remind you to kill me when we got home."

My father had two favorite lines that he would bellow at me. The first was, "Stop crying before I give you something to cry about."

The second was saved for spankings. He would ask that all-important Dad question, "Do you want some more?"

Ever the little smart aleck, I would look up at him and say, "Yeah, Dad, I can never get enough of a good whooping."

Dad's veins would pop from his neck as he tried to control his rage. I had challenged him. What would his reaction be? There were three options: he would spank me, lecture me, or laugh heartily.

Luckily for me, my Dad usually laughed.

Not all children are so fortunate.

Contained in this chapter are numerous stories kids told me of parents who not only rarely listened but seldom cared. ✪

Cheryl's father was the local sheriff, and her boyfriend was arrested for dealing pot. In their small Missouri town, everybody knows everyone else's business, so the gossip spread like a summer brushfire.

"My Dad does things I can't stand," Cheryl told me. "Like when my boyfriend calls, he'll say, 'Honey, it's your convicted felon on the phone.' He put a sign in my room that said, Home of Future Convicts of America. He leaves his handcuffs on my bed when he knows my boyfriend is coming over.

"If Daddy thinks he's going to scare me away from him he's crazy. I'm more committed to my boyfriend than ever. Daddy keeps hoping that someday I'll get the point, but a hammer is not as good a tool as a conversation. I just wish he'd talk to me about it. He thinks I can't have feelings. Guess I learned it from him."

Kids consistently say the following to me: They would rather have their parents beat them, hit them, punch them, or kick them than face the daily emotional abuse from Mom or Dad that leaves kids feeling small. Physical pain ends quicker. The scars of verbal abuse last and have a cumulative effect. And kids who face that sort of psychological scarring wonder why they're so unworthy of people's respect. ✪

On a trip through Texas, I came across a young rodeo rider. He told the students in his session that he was a barrel racer. He even had the bowed legs of a cowboy to prove it. But the young man was disturbed about something.

"My Dad keeps pushing me to be better. He keeps pressuring me everyday to practice. I like it and all but I can't stand the pressure. I finally snapped and told him I wanted to move back in with Mom.

"He said, 'You'll never be a champion if you move back with your mother."

"And I said, 'All I want to do is be a champion human being.

"My Dad started crying, and cowboys don't cry. He pushed me so hard that he pushed me away. I knew I had to go. I realized he did the same thing to Mom. He pushed her so hard she had to leave, too. He was just trying so hard to be the perfectionist."

Lao Tsu, the great Chinese philosopher said the following about leadership: "A leader is best when people barely know he exists, when his work is done, his aim fulfilled, they will say: we did it ourselves." ✪

Maria was a sixteen-year-old Filipino girl living in greater Los Angeles. She told me that she had a difficult time relating to her mother.

"My Mom's a nurse supervisor and she's constantly talking to me in medical terms. I'd say, 'Mom, I had a fight with my best friend, Cheryl.' And she say things like, 'Maybe it's time to change the sheets or you'll get bedsores. That's never going to heal if you just put a Band-Aid on it.

"The other thing is, that no matter what kind of problem I had, she'd start yelling at me that life has bigger problems. Then she'd tell me about some baby on the hospital floor who is dying of spina bifida and struggling for every breath. Or the woman who has to have her leg removed from cancer, or the young man who had a portion of his cheek removed from chewing tobacco. She goes on and on and on about these people who are suffering. Finally I said, 'Mom! Everything isn't an ER episode!'

"I think she deals so much with people's bodies that she forgets about their soul. She can't deal with emotions. Maybe it's because my father left us and she put all of herself into her work. But I'm just not sure she cares about me."

I defended Maria's mother, saying that she obviously had to work extremely hard to make ends meet. In doing so, that left her mother with very little extra time for Maria. "Her hard work pays for everything you own," I said.

"I guess so," said Maria "But it doesn't cost anything to listen to me." ✪

I held a forum at a school in Casper, Wyoming. Unemployment was rampant because oil jobs, once so plentiful and lucrative, had vanished. I heard from a teenage girl who I'll call Lydia. She had strawberry blonde hair, and her cute face was dotted with freckles. She looked like a character from a Norman Rockwell painting.

Lydia complained about her father. He boasted that he never had to lay a hand on his kids. Yet he called them useless and losers and scum and lowlifes. I call that kind of abuse 'emotional leukemia.' It wears away at a child's spirit.

In fact, Lydia had lost all spark. In the brief time I spoke to her, she seemed devoid of *joie de vivre*. In an attempt to cheer her mood, I said, "Did you know that a face without freckles is like a sky without stars?"

Those kind words - a simple compliment - made her burst into tears. It went beyond typical crying, though, so I asked what was wrong.

Lydia said, "Nobody ever says anything nice to me. My father does nothing but make me feel horrible about who I am and what I do. He's never said anything nice to me. Sometimes I lie in bed and pray that he won't come in and tell me how bad my grades are or how ashamed he is of me. I think it's because his father treated him that way. And I don't ever want to have kids because of that."

I told her that she should choose to break that cycle. She had the knowledge to avoid abuse of her own kids, if she ever had any. Then I told her about my own mother, who was an alcoholic. I loved my mom very much, but I didn't like her behavior. She was hard on me and was little help when it came to my self-esteem. She said things that hurt my feelings, and I was a pretty sensitive person. But the thing I discovered was that when someone doesn't encourage you, you have to encourage yourself. You have to learn to become your own best friend. ✪

Both of David's parents were police officers, and that may have been the source of his rebellious nature. When David was fifteen, he stole his mother's van and drove to Florida to visit his girlfriend. He was arrested while trying to rent a cheap hotel room. (The proprietor mistakenly thought David was trying to solicit a prostitute.)

"How do you think you made your parents feel?" I asked him.

"They had to report their own son to the station and search for me," David said. He hung his head in shame. "I guess that put them in an embarrassing situation. My Mom bought an airline ticket and flew down to get me. I know I humiliated them."

"But how do you think they felt about your disappearance?" I asked. "Don't you think they were scared because they couldn't find you?"

"Yeah, I know they care about me, and I know they were real happy I was alive. I'm lucky they aren't using me for target practice."

I asked how his parents dealt with the situation.

"They made me get a job and pay for everything; my Mom's airline ticket, the money to bail me out."

"What did you learn from this?" I asked.

"I learned I wasn't in love with that girl as much as I thought," he answered. "And I learned that my parents care for me, even though they piss me off that they're cops."

Teenage rebellion is every parent's burden, but it can be minimized through communication. Don't wait for your child to act out. Open the lines of communication now and let them vent their frustrations. Then listen to every word, even if it hurts you to do so. It's better to release emotions and come to understandings than to let negative emotion s fester. Communication is one of the best ways to avoid regrets. ✪

I heard this funny line from a young man in Berkeley, California, the bastion of Sixties radicalism:

"My Mom and Dad grew up in Berkeley, and they were exactly the kind of people they don't want me to hang out with now." ✪

In New Jersey, I met a young African American girl, Tanya, who admitted that she plays basketball to let off steam when her parents get on her nerves.

"I learned it from my Dad," she said. "I think the hardest thing to go through is when your parents get divorced. My Mom who's always angry now says, 'You deal with things just like your Father.'

"I told her, 'Mom you're just all pissed off because you can't dunk like Dad and I can.' Mom laughed about it."

I was impressed at how this young girl had chosen to deal with the situation. Humor was a good way to get her mother to see the point.

"Yeah," Tanya said, "but it was really hard for me to get to that place. I had to listen to each of them talk about each other like a dog, and you just don't know what to do. And when my Mom would get mad at me, she'd say I was acting all like him. Now, how am I going to fix that? I came from both of them. It just left me feeling numb because there was nothing I could do about it."

I told her that she was helping her Mom see what she was doing by acting as the parent in their family situation. "You must love her a lot to do that," I said.

"Yes, I do," Tanya replied.

While children are a reflection of the people who raise them, it's important to see your child as a unique individual, especially in their teenage years. ✪

Sometimes, kids at tough urban high schools are the hardest to get through to. Trying to get them to feel more compassion for each other as human beings and less like targets on their tough streets is no easy task. So when I met Marvin, a charismatic guy who was throwing funny lines at me right and left, I needed him on my side to help the rest open up.

"Marvin, how do you think your Mom feels when you get brought home in a police car because you won't stay in school?" I asked.

"I tell you, Big Mike, I could be on the street in any town. Dangerous streets, with gang bangers, wanna-be gang bangers, drug dealers, armed robbers, and car thieves. None of them make me afraid. But what really send shivers up my spine - having my Momma find out something about me that I didn't want her to find out.

"She'd kick my ass, then call over her sisters to kick my ass. These are not little women. For half my life, I thought my name was 'Damned Fool!' These are church buffet women who dress real nice on Sunday but if I do something bad, my Momma will put on a sweat suit to kick my ass. She goes to the sporting good store and buys an oar and makes Auntie hold me down."

Marvin seemed to hit a nerve with a lot of kids in the room. Some of the other boys started to admit that their Momma would beat them too if they got caught up in gang activities.

After we all caught our breath from laughter, I asked him, "Marvin, what has this fear of your Momma done for you?"

"It made me more steady. She's my center of gravity. See, I don't got a Daddy, I got a paddle. But I know what's right and wrong and a lot of people on my streets have no one to care about them enough to tell them what's right and wrong. Even though I'm scared as hell of her sometimes, I know she doing the right thing 'cause I ain't in nearly as much trouble as some other kids I know." ✪

I asked a group of San Francisco students, "What would you most like to tell your fathers?"

A young Chinese-American boy said, "My father has abandoned the family for business. He works everyday until late at night. I never hardly see him anymore. He keeps saying how he's making all this money for us. This is not who he was. I used to spend a lot of time with him. It's depressing to all of us to watch him make business more important than us." The boy broke down in tears.

Next to him sat a quiet, hardnosed black kid named Daryl who caught me by surprise with his gut-wrenching story. The vibrato in his voice belied his normally tough exterior.

"I'd like to tell my father to get off the crack pipe. He had a gun at my Grandmother's head. She's the one that takes care of us all. I was so mad at him. I'd like for him to get into a treatment program 'cause he's sick."

"Have you ever tried to tell him how you feel?" I asked.

"No," Daryl said. "I got no respect left for him. My job now is to help my Grandmother look after my little brother."

"It's hard when you have to become the parent, isn't it, Daryl?"

"Yes, it is, Mr. Pritchard. I am never going to let me or my little brother do crack."

Put in that perspective, the Chinese boy's problem didn't seem nearly as severe, yet his sadness, too, was just as valid. Both boys needed their fathers, yet neither of them could count on their Dads.

Ninety percent of the kids that I meet across America just want their fathers to listen to them. I see a great father hunger out there. ✪

E veryone picked on me because they said I was gay," young Franklin said. "They called me names."

"What kind of names?" I asked.

"Faggot, homo, queer."

"Why do you think they call you that?"

"Because I'm skinny and because my Momma needs me," he said. "I got to get home after school, and I can't stay out with the other kids."

"Why does your Mom need you?"

"She gets drunk, and I gotta take care of her so she don't hurt herself. Nobody else wants to do anything with me. She's all I got. So I watch TV with her so neither of us has to be alone."

"If your Mom was here right now, what would you like to tell her?"

Franklin thought it over and said, "I'd like to tell my mother to not get drunk so much. Ever since my little brother died, she's been burying the pain in a bottle." ✪

My oldest boy, Connor, is a gifted athlete who enjoys sports more than his old man ever did. After one soccer game, he got in the car frustrated and pissed off.

"That was a great game," I said trying to make him feel better.

Angrily, he spouted, "Did you see that kid Ian trip me on purpose? He kept punching me and kicking me and they never called a foul on him!"

"But Connor, you scored on him three times."

"I still hate that kid's guts."

"You played it the right way. You didn't hurt him back, and you just played harder than him."

"I still hate his guts."

"You know, Connor," I said, "I think Ian's parents are going through some hard times."

Connor's face screwed up with frustration, and he said, "Dad, can I just hate the kid for five minutes before you tell me what a sad home life he has?"

Okay, so I take my job home with me just like every other Dad. I was looking at the other kid's pain and not at the anguish of my own son. I wasn't listening to him. ✪

There's a group home in Nebraska for boys who have been in-carcerated for various reasons. I was called in to speak to the young men, all of them sixteen or seventeen years of age. Fighting had broken out at the home among the boys, and sometimes they were extremely violent.

Most of the kids I meet in group homes of late have either alco-holic/drug-addicted parents or the children are learning disabled. I'm sure that these aren't the only causes for the kids' frustrations and anger, but they're the reasons I hear most often.

A boy named Mike with glasses and scruffy blonde hair seemed to be isolated from the others. When I talked to him, I sensed that he was highly intelligent. He could produce brilliant answers to my questions and still remain aloof. I asked him, "You seem to know a lot about the world, Mike. Are you a great reader?"

"I'm dyslexic."

"How have your parents dealt with your dyslexia?" I asked.

"The typical teenage way."

"What does that mean?"

"NOT!" he answered. His rage was as palpable as a blast of hot wind.

"Do you think you have anger in you?"

"Yeah…Doesn't everybody?"

"How did you deal with it at home?" I asked. Suddenly, the other boys burst out laughing. "What's so funny?" I asked.

"I burned my house down," Mike said in an unsettlingly calm voice.

"You burned your house down?" I leaned in very close to him, purposely invading his space. I could see he'd put up a very hard front.

With heavy cynicism, he replied, "Yeah, I want to be a fireman."

The group laughed uproariously. But not me. I turned gravely serious.

"You can't be fireman if you're an arsonist, Mike. What hurt you so bad that you wanted to burn your house down? You started a fire. That's a cry for help."

The boy stared at the floor and wouldn't meet me eye to eye.

"That's a cry for water," another boy wisecracked.

"I'm not talking to you," I snapped. That silenced the group. I knew that Mike had been hurt tragically. He desperately needed to talk about it to get past his pain. I drew closer to him still and said, "They were hurting you at home, weren't they, son?"

The tears were slow in coming, but within seconds the dam burst.

Once you get them to cry, you're inside them. They're vulnerable. They have to admit their emotions because all eyes are on them. If he or she knows you care, the words will tumble out. The soul has to be healed. No human can hold as much pain as was emanating from this child.

"It was my stepfather," Mike whispered.

"Your stepfather hurt you in the worst way," I said.

He slid his glasses up on his forehead and rubbed his reddened eyes. The group fell painfully quiet. Mike said to me under his breath, "I thought you were a comedian, not Sigmund Freud."

"I think he's both," said the wisecracker, but with a serious tone.

Mike's good friend leaned into him. "Just tell him. He's not going to tell anybody. He's no policeman."

Mike opened up. "Yeah, he hurt me. Really bad. That's why I started the fire. That way I didn't have to admit it, but I knew I'd get help without ratting out my parents."

The poor young man wanted love from his parents so desperately that he'd sooner burn his house down than admit to having been sexually abused.

Kids' eyes will sometimes send signals from their heart. We need to take time to read them and interpret them. ✪

Isn't it ironic that we give licenses to barbers and hairdressers, testing them on whether or not they have the relatively rudimentary skill to cut hair, yet anyone can have a child? ✪

I knew a man who collected a quarter of a million dollars worth of beer steins. They were impressive and beautiful beer steins from all over the world. Some were gold, silver, ceramic, and all sizes and shapes. His rathskellar was crammed full of them. But because of his obsession, the collector had no time for his children. He practically ignored them.

His kids grew up so angry at their father that, when the man died, they sold his entire beer stein collection on their front lawn in a yard sale…for a penny apiece. ✪

Lea was a beautiful and intensely shy girl who told me she couldn't wait to leave her Montana home. I asked why.

"Because I hate my mother."

"Did she do something to hurt you?" I asked.

"Nothing I ever do is right. I'm sixteen years old, but my mother won't let me do the dishes because she's sure I'm going to break something. I wrote her a Mother's Day card once and she circled all my spelling errors in red. I wanted to take a photography class at school, but she wouldn't buy me a camera because she said I would lose it. She hated all my friends and told me all these things about their family and told me they weren't good enough to be in our house. Now, I have nobody. And the sad thing is, if you just drove by our house you'd think it was completely normal."

"What does your father do?" I asked.

"He does whatever my mother tells him to do."

"Can you talk to her? Can you tell her how you feel?"

Lea cried and said, "She'd probably tell me that I wasn't good at expressing my feelings. I'm sick of it. I just want to run away."

I told Lea that she needed to talk to someone. Everyone is entitled to his or her feelings. I explained that by sharing emotions, people understand you better. I suggested that she get help from a school counselor or some other adult so she would know that she wasn't alone. Then maybe she could help her mother.

Parents need to make a paradigm shift from controlling to understanding. A good parent is not a controller as much as he or she is a guide; not a person who's in the boat rowing with the child but someone who teaches how to steer. A good parent helps his or her child find the wind in the sails that they need to navigate their own course. Kids don't want parents who control where they go, but you have to let them know they always have a safe harbor to return to no matter how rough the storm. ✪

In the early 1970s, a pregnant girl came to me in distress. She was from a steadfastly Catholic family, and her parents were pillars of the community. Not only was she a pregnant teenager, the boy who was responsible was black. Her parents were horror-struck. Their religious beliefs forbade such behavior, and interracial relationships were still taboo.

As thoughtfully and gently as I could, I chided the girl about her sexual promiscuity in an effort to save her from having that happen again. But her parents were so angered that they abandoned their daughter emotionally. How, they wondered, could she possibly do this to them? They made a scene, disowning her and stigmatizing her as if she was a witch and they were righteous Puritans. It seemed odd to me that such religious people would be so unforgiving. Their judgment was terribly twisted.

I tell people, without any intention of offending the true believers, that religion is for people who are afraid of going to hell, and spirituality is for people who've already been there. Some pious people are more interested in fire insurance for their souls than they are in doing the right thing.

The girl's parents were abandoning her out of their idea of tough love, but it was misguided. They refused to admit that the true source of their humiliation was that they used to ridicule the kind of people who wound up in such circumstances. They needed a dose of humility; or as they say in Central American, 'Get down off your horse and walk with the people.'

Fortunately for the girl, the boy responsible for getting her pregnant was upstanding and honorable. He did the right thing. He assured me that he would take full responsibility as an adult. He did just that. He also went on to college and graduated.

The girl became a corporate leader in St. Louis. And I believe the reason for her success in business comes from the fact that she doesn't judge people. She hires many students from continuation schools – kids who were thrown out of other schools because of bad behaviors, including teenage pregnancies.

Paradoxically, the devoutly Catholic parents divorced shortly after the baby was born. To them, it was tragic, like a death in the family.

One of the greatest insights in life is that we all make mistakes. The blessed people understand and forgive. ✪

One day, I sat outside my lodge accommodations in Juneau, Alaska, admiring the Mendenhall Glacier with a middle-aged man named Stuwash. I was freezing, but I sat patiently as the Inuit man talked to me. The topic was parenting, but for some reason he suddenly segued into a tale about an eagle.

"You know, the eagle is sacred to my people. I had an eagle once that was wounded. It had hurt its wing. I knew it would claw me if I came close to it, so I covered it with a blanket. Then I cut a hole in the blanket for its head.

"It was a big eagle, and I let it mend at my cabin. I put a poltice on its wing to help it heal. Everyday, I hunted mice or rabbits to feed the bird. Eventually, he got stronger.

"Finally, one day, I knew the eagle was all better. But he just wasn't flying. I think he got too fat from me taking care of him. I couldn't get him to shoo. So I tied a piece of rope on his leg and tried to make him fly, but he only got irritated at me and tried to claw me. So I put him back into the blanket and climbed a mountain with him.

"When we reached the top, I threw him right off of the mountain. And then he flew. He circled once, looked at me, and then was gone.

"I went back to my cabin and was reading a book when it dawned on me that it was time to feed the bird. I got up from my chair, then realized he was gone."

Stuwash stared at me for several seconds, waiting to see if I comprehended. All I could say was, "Wow, he was gone, huh?"

"You're missing the point," Stuwash said.

I grinned and asked, "Okay, what's the point?"

"That's what it's like to be a parent. You feed them until they're too fat and don't want to fly. And then you try to make them leave, and they won't leave. They try to hurt you. It isn't until you kick them off the mountain that they leave. Then you miss them when they're gone." ✪

"You may give them your love but not your thoughts, for they have their own thoughts... You may strive to be like them, but seek not to make them like you."

Kahlil Gibran "The Prophet"

The Pain of Insults

"Nobody can make you feel inferior without your consent."
Eleanor Roosevelt

In my high school days, we'd gather on the steps of the Garrison family's front porch and verbally cut each other down for fun. We called it 'capping.' The Garrison brothers were built like refrigerators with heads, and they could intimidate anyone with sheer muscle. If they grew horns, they'd have been mistaken for cattle. And they were definitely not rocket scientists. They were the kind of guys who laughed raucously at the Three Stooges until their faces turned red, and they'd slap each other every time Curly got punched in the face. Not the sharpest tools in the shed. For me, they were easy targets because when it came to clever comedic lines, I outwitted the Garrison brothers every time.

We'd laugh and insult each other for hours with lines like:

"Nice shirt. Somewhere there's a Chevy without seat covers."

"You're so smart, you think Cheerios are donut seeds."

"I bet you thought that Polynesia is what happens when parrots forget things."

Kids do the same thing today. When they 'cap' or 'tag,' the target is usually someone's Mama.

"Your Mama is so fat, her rear end has it's own senator."

"Your Mama is so fat that Earl Scheib Auto paints her toenails."

"Your Mama is so fat that when she wore her Malcolm X t-shirt, a helicopter wanted to land on her."

Where I grew up, there was a heavyset girl named Gina who nearly everyone constantly tormented. I was no exception. The poor girl would try to pass through the school halls and make it to her locker without being noticed. The Garrison brothers made her their special target.

"Hey Gina, nice legs," one of the brothers would say, "Last time I saw legs like that was in the circus."

"Your skirt looks like a billboard for scotch tape!"

Then they would bellow this sophomoric song: "Gina, Gina round and fat/ Could not see where her feet were at/ When she skipped rope on the ground/ The earth would shake for miles around." Everyone laughed except Gina. She bowed her and walked away. I could have easily insisted that the Garrison brothers stop or I would tell everyone their math grades. Instead, I laughed, too.

Jump ahead many years later. I was working in juvenile hall and a violent kid swiped at me with a knife, wounding my head. Stitches were required. I lay in the emergency room where a beautiful doctor treated me. I flirted with her, doing my best to impress the lovely woman. She picked up my chart and said my name aloud.

"Michael Pritchard. I remember you."

"Oh? Have you seen me perform somewhere?" I asked.

"I'm Gina, Gina Mangiardi," she said.

My jaw dropped like an anchor. Here was that chubby girl who I had tormented as a boy, and she had become a gorgeous woman. I wanted to dig a big hole to crawl into. For the first time in my life I was at a loss for words.

When I gathered the nerve to speak, I stammered, "Gina, I can't believe it. You're so beautiful. I mean, you know, we were awful to you. I'm so sorry."

She smiled, tugged the stitch in my head, and then spoke seriously. "At first, it hurt real bad, but I wasn't going to let a bunch of idiots ruin my life. I studied hard and became a doctor."

She left the room, and I was overcome with shame. The consequences of our verbal abuse of that poor young girl never occurred to us. We were just amusing ourselves, glad to be the tormenters and not the tormented. I was so sorry for all the times I could have stopped the Garrison brothers but laughed instead. Gina returned with a smile, handed me a prescription, and sent me on my way.

When I got to the drug store, the pharmacist asked a question about my prescription. He said that there were two doctor's notes. The first was pain medication, but the second one appeared to be of a personal nature. He showed me, and I read what Dr. Gina had written.

"Michael's brain was very small/

Although he was almost 10ft. tall/

Now I'm thin and he got fat/

Ha, ha, ha, it goes like that!"

I definitely had that coming to me. And here's the lesson: Your kid can choose to be a victim or choose to be a bully, but whatever they choose they need to realize that, at any time, the roles can switch. ✪

It's ironic that a naval weapons base would be located in the middle of a desert, but that's the case with the China Lake Station in California's Mojave Desert. I was asked to speak to the children on the base, young sons and daughters of American military personnel. On my arrival, it took over thirty minutes to clear security, which is not unusual, especially in these troubled times.

After giving my speech, a diminutive, sixth-grade black girl approached me. She said, "My father is a naval aviator. And my father is my hero. And my father is a good man. And I'm sick and tired of the word nigger." She then began to cry.

Contrary to what you might think, bigotry is just as rampant on military bases as it is anywhere. With all of the integration in the armed forces, you might guess that it's less prevalent. Unfortunately, kids hear that offensive word even on our military installations.

I told that little girl and her classmates that there are too many African-American heroes in our navy, too many African-American heroes in our country, too many African-American heroes in our history, and too many good African people in our world for that word to ever be used. You have to confront those who say that word and tell them never to use it again.

When I finished, the little girl with the tears in her eyes said, "Excuse me, but could you say that to the black kids as well?" ✪

I visited Beckley, West Virginia, a city near the Appalachian Mountains just an hour's drive south of the capital, Charleston. I spoke to high school students there, and I asked if anyone would like to share with the group what it felt like to be left out.

A short girl rose to address everyone. She wore black camouflage pants, and her unusually long black hair obscured her face. When she brushed away her locks she exposed her disfigured upper lip.

She said, "Y'all call me retard because I have a cleft palate. Everyone teases me about it. It's been really hard for me. But I have a 4.2 grade point average, and a 140 IQ, and a full scholarship to Western Kentucky or Berea College, whichever I choose.

"I looked up the word retard in the dictionary, and it means slow in progress or growth or mentally incapacitated. Neither of those has anything to do with me.

"But I can tell you what stupid is. It's a bunch of hicks and hillbillies in a small town leaving some poor child totally isolated because her lip is different."

When she finished her stirring speech, the entire student body of over 150 kids rose in unison to give her a standing ovation. The applause surprised her, and the girl burst into tears.

Later, the principal took me aside and said with a grin, "Y'know, I believe she wrote that speech a ways back and was just waiting on you to come and introduce her."

I told that principal what a child once told me, "When you find your voice, you've found your soul." ✪

More than a year after the tragedies at the World Trade Center in New York and the Pentagon, I gave a performance at a Pleasanton, California school. Afterward, I asked if any of the kids wanted to speak out about any teasing they had received from others. A thoughtful, young Sikh boy wearing a turban walked to the front of the group.

"My name is Omed, and you make fun of me, and you call me the Afghan kid. And you pick on me and you hurt me. I don't deserve this. Listen..." Omed hesitated to make his point. "I am as upset as any of you about what happened on 7-11."

All of the kids in the room burst out with laughter at Omed's obvious blunder. Then some of them began imitating the cartoon character on the Simpson's who owns the convenience store.

I chastised them sternly. "Hey, you all know he meant nine-eleven. Now stop." That quieted the children.

Later, a pudgy boy with thick glasses that made him look like a hoot owl approached me. He sounded like a miniature Joe Pesci. "Okay, I bought what you were saying about emotion and not picking on others, but when you stifle us, it's just not fair. I mean, that kid had a bonehead moment. We should be allowed to laugh at a bonehead moment."

There's an old expression. Comedy is when the wind blows a man's hat off his head and he has to chase it down the street. Tragedy is when it's your hat. That's a valuable lesson for kids. ✪

A school counselor called me to her quiet little town in Montana to meet a girl who desperately needed help. Tiffany was a sixteen-year-old who had been severely isolated from her peers, and she had attempted suicide. I traveled as soon as my schedule permitted.

I arrived after lengthy traveling, and my stomach was making noises like a grizzly bear in heat, so I wolfed down a gigantic roast beef sandwich. As luck would have it, young Tiffany showed up just at that moment, so I stuffed the entire sandwich into my mouth. What can I say? I can't help myself.

The stunningly pretty blonde said hello, and I pointed to my bulging cheeks before speaking. I chewed as fast as I could and imitated a gorilla by pounding my chest. She smiled, and I knew I would be able to reach her.

"Nice to meet you, Tiffany," I said. "Sorry, but there's no way I was going to share my sandwich."

We chatted politely, and she shared information about her family, all of which seemed quite normal to me. I got to the point.

"Your counselor says you're all alone. Can't you talk to your friends?"

"Friends?" Tiffany said. "I have no friends."

"Why not?"

"Because they all hate me."

"Who hates you?"

"Everybody. The whole school."

"Isn't there anyone you can talk to?" I asked. "A girlfriend? A guy who's a friend?"

"I have no friends. No guy would even talk to me. They all started saying that I had herpes. The whole school spread the rumor. Even girls I thought were my friends. Do you know what it feels like to walk down the hall and hear nothing but whispers behind your back? So I started acting all tough. Make them think like what they were saying didn't bother me. It made me sick to my stomach to hold it all in. One night, I begged my Mom to let me stay home from school, but she said I had to go. I went in the bathroom and threw up. The thought of everybody just looking at me walk down the halls and whispering was too much. I couldn't take it anymore. I took my Dad's razor and cut my wrists. But it wasn't deep enough, so I just bled all over everything."

She showed me the scars on her wrists.

Tears streamed down her pale cheeks like water from a leaking faucet, and she said, "I'm a good person and I don't deserve this!"

I told her that she couldn't let people take away her personality, to make her be someone whom she knew wasn't.

"It just makes me so angry because it's not even true! I don't have herpes! I've never even had sex! This guy that I dumped started the rumor because I wouldn't have sex with him."

I asked if she stood up for herself and confronted the kids her were spreading the lies about her.

"Yeah, but they wouldn't believe me," she said. "Every time I even think about it, I start crying. Mr. Pritchard, this is a small town, and everybody knows everybody. I just don't have the guts to do it. I want to know if you'll do it for m."

At my request, Tiffany's counselor gathered thirty kids into a room. They included the main offenders of the gossip and the boy who initiated the rumor. The boys mostly wore plaid shirts and baseball hats. Most of the girls looked like Tiffany; they wore jeans and t-shirts. The students were seated in a semi circle around me, and the silent tension was as thick as mud.

I wasted no time and got to the root of the session. "A classmate of yours has been tormented so badly by some people in this school that she attempted suicide. She wants to know why you felt the need to spread a terrible rumor about her even though you knew it was isolating her?"

I could tell it was the right group to confront. Their shame was palpable, like a burst of cold air had entered the room. Remorse is a weighty feeling, and I could see it in their body language. Shoulders slumped. The boys' heads sunk. All of the girls' eyes misted. The only sound came from a girl openly sobbing at the back of the room.

I asked the crying girl if she knew which student I was referring to.

"Yes," the crying girl said. "I helped spread the rumor. It was fun at first, but I never thought it would get this far. I feel so bad for her."

The boy who had started the rumor sat with his arms crossed, and his face was blank.

A muscular jock named Brendan admitted, "I knew it wasn't true, but I did it anyway."

I asked why.

"Because everybody would think you're, like, some preppy kiss-ass if you stuck up for her."

"Who's going to say that about *you*?" I said as I pointed at his bulging muscles. "Look at you. I doubt you could be easily intimidated."

"I don't know. I guess I didn't think about the consequences."

A boy with acne who wore a baseball cap backwards admitted, "Sometimes you do shit like that because it's just easier than saying it's not true."

A girl named Shirl said, "Yeah, I did it too, and I know how it feels when people talk about you."

I asked how it made her feel when people talked about her.

"It hurt," she said in a whisper. A friend's comforting arm went around her.

I asked, "Why do we spread rumors about others when we know that it hurts when it happens to us?"

A girl with a pinched face and large glasses said, "Why are there all those magazines about the movie star lives? I think we're sick, and we like hearing bad stuff about people. Tiffany is pretty and always had tons a boyfriends, and I think I was probably jealous."

I pointed out that Tiffany's life had changed because of one lie. As a result, she had no friends and no relationships. Tiffany told me she hadn't had a date in three years because of the rumor. She was too embarrassed to even attend the session; that's how alone she was.

Suddenly, the macho boy who had started the rumor rose from his chair and, vainly trying to hold back his tears, left the room. Everyone fell silent.

To break the tension, a young man with bad acne and a clueless look on his face, piped up. "Hey, Mr. Pritchard. I'm a senior this year, and I just wanted to say, I don't have herpes but nobody has asked me out in three years, either."

The students exploded in laughter. Nobody laughed harder than me.

A football player slapped the back of the boy with the bad acne and said, "You hadn't counted on your ugliness factor."

A mixture of tears and laughter helped heal the situation.

Tiffany contacted me a few weeks later and said that some girls apologized. Other girls, however, just hung their heads in shame. Tiffany was pleased to say that she had a date with a guy and things were better.

She told me, "I still don't trust them like I did before this whole thing happened. I wish I had the courage to stand up for myself better. But I did learn one thing. Sometimes you can trust adults." ✪

I visited a group of schoolchildren and asked how many of them had ever used unkind words towards other students in the hallways. I wondered if anyone had uttered hurtful words like homo, fatso, chink, or retard. A number of kids shyly raised their hands. I glanced around the room and saw a boy with Down's Syndrome. He returned my gaze, smiled, and said, "Don't look at me!"

That deserved a hug. He was right. You'll never hear unkind words from a child with Down's Syndrome. It's ironic that some people consider them stupid. I think kids with Down's Syndrome are spies from God. ✪

Native Americans have wonderfully dry senses of humor. The best example comes from when I visited a Crow reservation in North Dakota. I spoke to kids there from various tribes; Crow, Northern Cheyenne, and Sioux.

I was waiting at the side of the road for my ride when a truck approached. The driver, a Native American man, stopped his vehicle and, without getting out, spoke to me.

"Are you the guy from television?" he asked.

"Do you mean John Goodman from *Roseanne*?" I said. Some people have mistaken me for that actor.

"No," the truck driver said. "I mean the guy who works with kids."

"Oh, yeah, that's me." I realized that he must have seen one of my Public Television programs.

The man looked at me and said, "You got fatter." Then he drove away.

Later, I spoke to the tribal chief. I told him that one of his men, a truck driver, insulted me. "He said I got fatter," I said in jest, hoping to get a chuckle out of him.

The chief, with his subtle, wry sense of humor, had me howling with laughter when he deadpanned, "He was not insulting you. He was giving you a Crow name." ✪

After finishing a speech to an assembly of students in Morgantown, West Virginia, I asked if anyone had questions. A large young man wearing a long black overcoat raised his hand. We'll call him Brett. He had a face thoroughly covered with pimples. Brett rose to his feet to confront his entire senior class. He spoke eloquently and loudly for everyone to hear.

"I've sat quietly for four years listening to everyone call me names. I don't have one friend. None of you people got to know me because I was fat and wore a black overcoat and had a bad complexion. I'm a good person, and I could have been a good friend to many of you. But you all stored in your mental computers the word 'loser' about me. And a lot of you wouldn't even reach out to me because of what people would say. Anywhere I went, I was always called a loser. I don't want anybody to feel ashamed, because when we're teenagers we're not good at that. But you should think about making friends with people who are different, because you never know who could become your best friend when you need it most."

The entire senior class gave him a standing ovation. The applause lasted several minutes. Their response may have been because they felt guilty about his accusations and maybe because he helped them grow up a bit that day. Or perhaps it was because everyone felt like Brett at certain times in his or her life, a bit victimized by the name-calling and isolated for no good reason.

I was dumbfounded by Brett's confidence and eloquence. He thanked me later for my words that inspired him, and I told him he had inspired me.

"I'm very glad you helped your classmates grow," I told him. "That was really brave of you to say how you felt, and I think you did some good." We talked at length, and I asked Brett if he had hobbies.

"I'm a highly skilled marksman with a long rifle," he said. "I can hit a spade from the middle of an ace of spades from 500 yards."

I did a double-take. There was no doubt in my mind that he was telling the truth. Then I laughed out loud and said, "Oh my God, I'm glad you didn't mention that at the assembly."

I knew that for whatever reason, good family, strong will or just the desire to not give in, that high school senior had not hurt anyone else with his pain. He was alone all those years and grew up from it. He became his own best friend and survived, and that was a truly noble accomplishment. ✪

The Chautauqua Institution is an exclusive non-profit enclave near Jamestown, NY, that has provided liberal arts education since 1874. It's a private community of talented artists and intellectuals. I spoke to an audience of the institution's most influential people, including teachers, parents, and children.

As I often do, I asked if there was a child who wished to express his feelings to the group. A thirteen-year-old boy came to the front of the room. He had spiked hair, earrings, and an eye ring. He wore a metal-studded choker around his neck and a black T-shirt with a rock band's logo. It read 'The World Sucks.'

The boy gave a bone-chilling speech. "You've all made fun of me, teased me, and tormented me. You just don't want to hear my pain. Because of that, you've triggered my anger. Now you'll have to learn to deal with that anger. I'm just telling everybody that for the last couple of months I've thought about killing myself. That wouldn't bother any of you. What do you care about my pain? But what you need to know is that sometimes, just sometimes, I sat around thinking of ways to take some of you with me."

That had an alarming effect on everyone in the room. One of the administrators, Mark, came to me and said, "I am, without any doubt, grateful that you're here at this time."

Most people might assume that the boy's punk attire was a statement or an act of rebellion. But sometimes kids dress outrageously as protection. They're reasoning is, 'People will leave me alone if they think I'm cuckoo.' Drawing out that boy's anger and listening to him may have prevented a regrettable act. ✪

I met Latosha at a session at an inner-city school in Newark, New Jersey. She wore a large Oakland Raiders football jacket that was at least two sizes too big for her, and her baseball cap was turned backward on her head.

I asked if any of the students were victims of persistent name-calling.

Latosha raised her hand. "Yeah, they call me Miss Piggy, Zit Face, Don King Hair, and the Beast."

"How does that make you feel?" I asked.

"I laughed when the boys teased me, but it really hurt inside."

"What did you do about it?" I asked.

"I learned to play the violin."

That surprised me. I asked her to tell us her story.

"I was born illegitimately. My Mom remarried a light-skinned man who didn't want to recognize me as his own. My Mom and step dad had two other children who they gave their focus to. My Mom was economically tied to my step dad. But he didn't respect me.

"One summer, I put on forty pounds. I had an interest in the violin, and even though I was very shy I went to talk to the music teacher. She told me, 'Obviously, a girl your size wouldn't look good behind a violin.'

"But I chose to play the violin because I loved it and because she said I couldn't do it. I built a soundproof room in my basement with glass windows so I could still watch my little brother and sister while I practiced. I practiced six to eight hours a day.

"In my senior year, I had an audition for one of the best music conservatories. I was so scared but knew if they were going to accept me they had to take me for me. I showed up in my Oakland Raiders jacket and announced to them I was from Newark, New Jersey. I knew they would never suspect a black girl from Newark would ever know Bach, so that's what I played. When I looked out into the audience after the first three bars, I knew I had that four-year scholarship. But that wasn't the important thing. My step dad was in the front row crying. I didn't know if he was crying because he was finally proud of me or because he was embarrassed for they way he had treated me all those years. But one thing I knew standing up there playing was that I had found myself, and nobody could ever take that away from me." ✪

> *"You have to stand up tall and walk tall.*
> *No one can ride your back when you're walking tall."*
> *Martin Luther King, Jr.*

Bullies

I often teach kids this simple message: When you're tired of being a bud, try to blossom. It's liberating for a kid when he or she finally gets an opportunity to vent and confront bullies. It creates a sense of empowerment.

A light-skinned black girl in Chambersburg, Pennsylvania, stood up in front of the entire student body at my request and explained what was upsetting her.

"I don't know what makes me the scapegoat. I don't know what's written on my face that says come and pick on me. But there are so many people in this school that have decided to make me the rag doll. I can't take anymore, and I'm close to death. Not because I'm going to kill myself. I'm just so worn down. I can't get up in the morning to get to school."

More often than not, any kid who's different from most becomes the lightning rod of taunts and teases. The bully's favorite victim is either the person who cries easily or the person who the bully can repeatedly make angry. Bullies love the kid who flips out at the slightest provocation. They learn the trigger words like "your momma" or something about the victim's personality or a physical abnormality. But when that child finally finds the forcefulness to stand up to the taunts, it's an awesome thing.

One example was an eighth grader I met in Fairfield, California. I asked her group if there was anyone who wanted to share what it was like to be teased. The girl raised her hand, but I could barely see her in the back of the room. My first thought was that she was awfully small for a thirteen-year-old. As she wheeled herself to the front of the room, I saw that she was in a wheelchair. She was an athletic girl with no legs.

She spun around in her chair to face the entire roomful of kids. With tight lips and a furrowed brow, she said, "I have no legs from an accident, okay? I've got a stepbrother at home who whacks me around and pushes me. And I've got two working class parents who don't talk to him about the way he treats me. So I've already got enough on my plate. I don't need anything else. Okay? So you need to know to leave me alone. If you don't like me, don't make fun or me or snicker at me. Just leave me alone. That's all I ask."

Then she promptly wheeled herself back to the rear of the room. But she stopped midway, spun around to face me, and in a gruff voice she said, "Thanks." Then she continued to the back of the room.

Anytime a young person is empowered to speak in front of his or her peers, it's the beginning of the freedom of their soul. The best gift to give a kid is to teach them to be a self-advocate. ✪

I met a girl at a California high school who was an Australian aborigine. She had lovely dark skin, thick black hair, and dazzling eyes. Her words to her classmates were powerful. There was little question that she was addressing the other schoolgirls on the way they treated her.

She stood before the entire school assembly and said in her rich Australian accent, "I'm a million miles away from home, and I miss it very much. It has been hard for me. Many of you have been kind and have reached out to me. But some of you have made my insides feel like broken glass."

That stunned the students. I hoped that the girls at the school took heed of what she said. For that girl, confronting her tormentors was one step towards lessening her anguish. ✪

After speaking to an assembly of students in New Jersey about bullying, they sent me wonderful letters. One young person told me that "you get to paint your own canvas with a letter." Here are a few.

Dear Mike,

Every day I come to school thinking that the people that made fun of me yesterday will leave me alone. When people make fun of me it is about my head being small, or I am too small, my ears being too big, that I am gay, that my clothes don't match, but I don't care about that, because I know that it is not true. They also say that I am stupid, retarded because I am in the resource room. It is hard enough at school but then I go home it is yelling, yelling, yelling. My parents are divorced and I don't get to see my dad that much and when I do I only get to see him for 2 days and 1 night or 5:30 pm to 9:00 pm. Some kids think that my life is just like theirs to be able to get to places. Example: One day I was playing soccer and a kid asked how rec. soccer was treating me and he had no idea what my life is about and how it is too hard to get around to get to the field to play. Those types of people should think of the other person and how they live before saying anything.

Thanks for the speech,
[name withheld]

Dear Mike P.,

People make fun of me they call me stupid, they say I have a rat nose. They say I have a rat nose because it is big they also call me snoz. They call me stupid because I hate to read. I'm in the lowest class because I hate to read I'm also a bad speller. I'm in the 2nd highest math class I'm good at math science and I'm ok at social studies, but I hate to read I can read but I hate it. I'm smarter than a lot of the people who call me stupid. My mom sent my sister to boarding school, it is called Hyde it is in Connecticut because she smoked a lot of things and stole. My mom pressures me to do better in school. She punishes me a lot I don't like it I do more than most people do at my age. She doesn't lend me any money and she won't let me get a job. My mom and dad are divorced I like spending time with my dad he is fun. My mom says that I shouldn't get involved with what goes on between them if it is my mom's fault, but if my dad does something wrong she makes sure that I know and then she tells her whole family how bad of a person he is. My mom and sister got in lots of violent fights using chairs as weapons and there [were] fists I always brake up those fights and I usually take a hit trying to stop them. My sister and I get into lots of fights also I have been stabbed with a screw driver and a knife before from my sister, she also hits me with brooms and other things, I've always been able to take more pain than most people I know, so I most of the time punch her after she does that to me. I get along real well with my dad; I can tell him most things that go on but not with my mom or my sister. I have a few good friends that I can tell anything to but most of them I can't. From,

[name withheld]

Dear Mr. Mike,

Thank you for coming to our school and talking about bullying. If you don't remember me, I'm the boy who came up and talked because people made fun of me having a high voice. I noticed that after the assembly people told me how brave and courageous I was to go up and talk to you.

People call me a faggot and gay. It hurts me so much and I don't like talking about it at home. That's why I had to go up and confront the 7th grade and tell them how I felt. I felt so relieved and relaxed after letting out my pain. So many people were so much nicer and kinder towards me and the other people who went up. Mrs. Burns told my parents what I did and they were enormously proud.

I have other friends who are made fun of. They also are in pain, but after that assembly they're relieved that someone actually understands what they're going through.

I express my feelings in acting. I am very interested in the arts. It helps take things off my mind such as bullying and peer pressure. I've been in many shows and plan to do more.

When I grow up, I want to be a psychologist. I want to help people with their problems and let them know there is someone who cares just like you do.

As you were speaking, I felt good because I know people with horrible home lives. They're made fun of because they're different. But the people who are making fun of them have just as horrible home lives as the people they're making fun of.

As I'm writing this letter, I think of all the wonderful things you've said and done for our school. You really touched my heart and helped our school know what we were doing was wrong.

Your friend, [name withheld]

Dear Mike,

Thank you for coming to our school and telling us about bullying and bringing up some of the people, because I teased every person that went up there and now I have more respect for them [than for] myself, and you also opened my eyes to show me that I was the fag not them.

Thank you for coming,
[name withheld]

A student once said to me, "You ever notice how bullies have a lot of followers but never any friends?"

Don't let your child be a follower to bullies.

And more importantly, never allow your kid to turn from a victim to a volunteer. ✪

No one had told me in advance of my speaking engagement at a rural California school that a tragic suicide had occurred just days earlier. I knew nothing about it until students informed me during our session. An eighth grade boy, tormented by other kids who called him 'faggot' and 'homo', wrapped himself in barb wire and jumped off the swing set. When I heard this, I was taken aback. I wasn't expecting to hear such a tragedy, especially not from that particular community, which was known as a bastion of liberalism.

With his shoulders slumped and his head hanging low, one young man stood up before the gathering of students and admitted his regret. "I'm deeply, deeply ashamed that I did that. I gave that boy self-doubt. We called him faggot and homo and queer, and he lisped and we made fun of the way he walked and he flipped his wrists and all. Well, a lot of kids here don't have the guts to admit it because they're holding it in, but I have to say it. I'll be ashamed till the day I die."

Later, I asked the adults for more details about the suicide. One of the teachers, whose long beard and hair made him look like a member of ZZ Top, told me that the child was "a deeply disturbed person," as if the students who tormented the boy had no culpability for what happened.

"Of course he was disturbed," I said, "if he was constantly being called fag and homo."

"No, it wasn't about that," the smug teacher said, completely convinced of his position. "He was definitely a disturbed kid."

He was so adamant that it made me angry. "You know what?" I said. "I think you're full of shit. You can lie to me, but I feel badly that you're lying to yourself. You have to say that to feel like it's okay. This community killed that child."

The teacher sneered, and as he walked away I heard him mumble dismissively, "Yeah. Outsiders."

Some people just can't face reality. Truth is a torch in a dark place. As the great Justice Louis Brandeis said, "Sunshine is the best disinfectant." ✪

When a bully stands up before his or her fellow students and apologizes, that's like an emotional avalanche. It happens surprisingly often in my work. I held a session with kids in Charleston, West Virginia, and a young man rose to speak to the crowd.

"I just want you all to know that I attend church every Sunday. I hear the sermons, and I sit and pray, and I read the scriptures with my family. But you know what? All of that's just words. It wasn't until today that I felt a sense of shame for the cruelty that I had put out. I had the power to intimidate because I'm bigger than everybody here and because I'm a football player and a wrestler. None of the stuff I learned in church was sinking in, until I saw you cry. And I realized that I was the person who made you feel bad, and I was the person who made you afraid to come to school."

A bully's tears come from the cellar of his soul. When you encourage kids to reach down deep and explore who they really are, revelations occur. ✪

In Iowa, at a session with eighth graders, I asked if anybody could readily admit to being a bully. I fully expected a boy to respond, yet none of the boys volunteered. Instead, a tall, pretty girl with glasses stood up. "I've been a bully," she said.

All of the teachers, students, and parents were surprised by her confession. She didn't seem the type. Everyone fell silent as the girl told her story.

"I've created relationships with other people. And all of them are my friends. But not out of love, not out of respect, and not out of wanting the best for me. It's out of fear of what I might do to them. It isn't a physical thing. It's about the fact that I would destroy them with words. And I would say things about them in a dark and mean and angry way. I now realize that none of them are my friends out of love. They're my friends out of fear. It's a very lonely place for me, and it must be a very lonely place for them. And I just woke up to that fact after listening to what was said here. I wanted to create that fear in them to get them to like me. I wanted them to be my friend for all the wrong reasons. And I apologize to the whole class for that."

Everyone in the room was astonished, including me. Her intellectual assessment was brutally honest. It was a stunning moment of truth, especially from an eighth grade student.

Fear is the little dark room where negatives are developed. Don't permit your children to use fear as the fulcrum in their relationships with others. ✪

I asked students at a New Jersey school if there was anyone among them who wanted to step forward and admit to being a bully. One tall, broad-shouldered senior with a husky voice stood before the assembly. He said, "I am the Frankenstein you created. Your hatred for me, your abuse of me, the way you picked on me. All I wanted for my whole time in high school was one friend. And I never got it. So I became a persecutor. I made you afraid of me and made you get out of my way in the halls. What you didn't know, and now you're hearing for the first time, all I wanted was a friend. Somebody to know me for who I really am. Someone who would know that I'm not really this kind of person."

Blaming others, however, for his behavior was not a fair judgment. That young man needed to look inside himself for the reasons behind his bullying. All he needed to do to attain friendship was to reach out and to be himself. As Elie Wiesel said, "When we die and go to Heaven, the only thing the Creator asks is, 'Why weren't you more yourself?'" ✪

I was in Terra Linda, California, speaking to grade school children about bullying. As I often do, I asked a student to come forward and speak to the gathering about her troubles. To my irritation, some kids began giggling as the girl spoke. Rising from my seat and glaring at the students, I spoke in a booming voice. "Stop! If you're sitting there with a smirk or if you're laughing while a child shares her pain, you go home and tell your Mommy and Daddy that Michael Pritchard was at your school, and he said that you're a sick, sick kid who needs to get some care or counseling. Tell Mommy and Daddy I said it, and if they don't like me talking to you like this, tell them to call me."

I then had the girl continue and the kids listened respectfully. When I finished with my session, the teacher said to the group, "I have spent my entire thirty years waiting, waiting, waiting for someone to say that to you kids. I didn't know the words that needed to be said. I just didn't know how to express myself. But when I watched Mr. Pritchard speak, that was my proudest moment of being a teacher."

While his sentiment touched me, I think all educators should speak out. Don't wait for someone like me to speak up for you. Teachers have to step up and not allow the fear of lawsuits to keep them from doing the right thing.

Teachers, when you see eleven year olds standing on the roof of a building, don't worry that Mommy and Daddy are going to sue you for lowering their child's self-esteem. Tell 'em, "Get off the roof, you knucklehead!" ✪

St. Dorothy's Rest is a cancer camp. I attend them occasionally to work and be with special kids who are cancer victims. We were on our way back to camp after a field trip at the beach. The man who drove the bus for us was a grumpy, Richard Nixon look-alike. He mumbled invectives and cursed as he drove the bus. He wasn't exactly a bully, but the conspicuously bitter man intimidated the kids.

I sat on the bus with a boy suffering from progeria, the rapid aging disease. He was a cute, cross-eyed little fellow who refused to let me leave his side, and I was happy to be with him. He kept hugging me and touching my face and giggling. Like most of the kids, he was under the age of ten. Eighty percent of them were suffering terminal illnesses. We all laughed and joked and had fun...which is what children in those dire situations need more than anything.

As we drove through the town of Occidental, I played a harmless trick on the bus driver. I did a pitch-perfect whistling imitation of a police siren. It sounded so much like an actual siren that the bus driver pulled over to the shoulder of the road.

All of the kids on the bus laughed with glee. The priest who accompanied us shot me a scolding glance. "Please don't do that anymore, Michael."

"Okay, Father Kevin," I said. I couldn't understand why he was so perturbed by my harmless practical joke.

"You don't understand," Father Kevin whispered to me. "This man behind the wheel is a very angry fellow."

The bus driver pulled away unaware of what had happened. Then the boy on my lap, as cute and sweet as a puppy, looked at me with his crossed eyes and whispered, "Do it again."

How could I resist?

My second siren imitation was as convincing as the first, and the bitter bus driver pulled over once again. The kids laughed even harder. But this time the driver caught on. He shifted the bus into park, rose from his seat, and stomped to the back of the vehicle where I sat.

"I have a responsibility to the people on this bus!" he bellowed. He even sounded like an irate Richard Nixon, jowls flapping as he spoke. "And I do not appreciate you people making distracting noises like that!"

All of the kids pointed at me and said, "Mike did it."

I laughed and said, "Remind me to never rob a bank with you guys."

Once the bitter bus driver returned to his duty, Father Kevin begged me to apologize to the man. When we reached our destination and all of the kids were taken off the bus, I approached the driver. With my hands full of swim gear, I said, "Listen, I apologize if that disturbed you. The kids and I were just having some fun."

Grumpy Nixon closed the bus doors so the children couldn't hear. Then he said, "Hey, you know what? You know what? Fuck you."

He was so comically over-the-top in his anger that I burst out laughing. I stumbled off the bus holding my stomach with laughter. It was pure absurdity that a man surrounded by beautiful dying children could be so detached from their lives and so involved in no one else but himself. I was genuinely sorry, but he didn't want to hear it.

When I rejoined the kids, they asked, "What did he say?"

I said through my laughter, "He just wanted to thank us all for such a fun bus drive."

I still laugh my head off thinking of Grumpy Nixon, but his vitriol offers a lesson for all adults.

Have a sense of humor. Young people can be a constant source of delight if you take pleasure in their growth. Guide them with joy.✪

In March 2003, I drove to Stockton, California to participate in a conference in which I asked grade school students to speak out about bullying. As I approached Lifeseeds Christian Church where the conference was held, I was struck by a dizzying sense of déjà vu, as strong as if a hot dry breeze had hit me. I quickly realized that I had visited that location before. The church was near Cleveland School, which was the site of a devastating massacre fourteen years earlier. I had returned to the site of tremendous heartbreak.

My mind wandered back to 1989. Stockton was in the news due to a horrific school shooting. Patrick Edward Purdy, 26, ran amok in the elementary school with an automatic weapon. For lack of a better term, he was a nutcase who kept tiny toy soldier figurines scattered around his hotel room. Wearing paramilitary clothing, Purdy calmly entered the school he had attended 15 years earlier and shot over 35 children and at least one teacher. Five victims died. He then took his own life. The tragedy stunned the nation and haunted the city. Two days later, I went there to counsel the surviving students and teachers.

Many of the kids who attended Cleveland School at that time were Vietnamese, Mung, and Cambodian. Their parents had fled Southeast Asia for America in the 1970s in the hope of escaping the war and violence of their respective countries. It was tragically ironic that they had to face even more misery one decade later.

I remember asking the second and third graders what we could do to help them feel safe in school and to help the community at large. A tiny boy with jet-black hair raised his hand to answer, and with an impish grin – God bless him – he said, "Make sure that guy's family isn't allowed to come over here, either."

We all let out a cathartic laugh. The boy knew exactly what impact his statement would have, and he succeeded. I was so grateful for that funny, touching moment. ✪

Someone to Hear Their Sad, Sad Secrets

*It's odd that you can get
so anesthetized by your own pain
or your own problem
that you don't quite fully share
the hell of someone close to you.*
Lady Bird Johnson

When I was a medic treating critically wounded soldiers in Viet Nam, I was taught that you shouldn't talk to the wounds. Instead, you must talk to the spirit. I was never a great medic, but I learned how to restore a person's humanity. The wounds will heal. People can function without a limb, without an eye, without certain organs. But you can't function with a depleted spirit. Unless someone throws you the life preserver of self-worth, you'll drown in an ocean of despair.

The truth is that many children are drowning in despair but don't have the emotional wherewithal to holler for help. So they keep secrets bottled up inside. Sometimes all they need is someone willing to listen.

I held a session with a group of schoolchildren in rural Alabama. Once we were all settled in, I asked who among them had any responsibilities at home. A young African American boy named Taylor was quick to raise his hand.

"I have a responsibility that when my Daddy gets drunk and starts beating on my Mom that I take the baby and hide him in the closet so Dad doesn't hurt the baby."

I wasn't ready for that. It was my very first question, and his answer floored me. But the boy clearly needed to get that off of his chest immediately. I asked Taylor why he decided to share that information.

"Mike, everybody needs to meet a kind stranger to tell their secrets to." ✪

I met a bitter young man in Iowa, who I'll call Jeremy. The fifteen-year-old was teeming with rage and lashed out at his teacher. As a result, the teacher argued with him vehemently and was very judgmental towards Jeremy. I was allowed to meet with him privately in the teachers' lunchroom at his high school.

Lowering my voice to a near whisper, I asked Jeremy what made him so angry. "What's hurting you so badly?"

He blinked his eyes with surprise as if no one had ever asked him that question before. Jeremy gazed at his shoes and softly said, "Well, I'll tell you what's hurting me. I've got a mother who's tied to this guy, and we're in this trailer, and the guy comes into my room at night and touches me. He puts his fingers inside me, and I have to take that."

I've heard that sort of admission too many times from kids, yet it never fails to shock me. Pity filled my heart. Tears brimmed in my eyes. "Have you told anyone about this?" I asked.

His caustic reply was, "Yeah. You. Now."

"Anybody would be angry if that was happening to them," I said.

Jeremy lowered his head. "We can't get out. We got no money."

I said, "That doesn't mean he's allowed to do that to you."

"I know," he said, "but what can I do? My Mom needs that guy."

I said, "No, you don't need him. We have to take care of this."

He looked at me pleadingly and shook his head. "Now that you've told me, I have an obligation to see that he's arrested."

"But what's my Mom going to do?" he asked.

"I have to look out for you right now," I replied. "I don't want that man doing that to you anymore or to anyone else. Chances are, he'd done it before to other kids."

Jeremy crumpled like a marionette with its strings cut. His rage evaporated.

I contacted the sheriff's department and Child Protective Services to handle the boy's case. Charges were brought against the man who molested Jeremy.

I watched his teacher's face when she received the news about Jeremy's molestation. She held tremendous disdain for the boy, but her face melted with pity when the principal explained the details to her. She seemed to realize in that moment that she wasn't helping her pupil at all. She was perhaps only making matters worse for him by being cynical to his anger.

As Mother Teresa said, if you spend your time judging people, you won't have time to love them. ✪

In the Appalachian Mountains in West Virginia, historic coalmining territory, I encountered a handsome young man named Robert. He impressed me profoundly. Robert was among a group of teenagers at a school I visited. I asked the kids, "Who here has responsibility at home?"

Robert raised his hand and spoke. "My Father was killed in a coal mining accident. My Mother passed away of a heart attack at 44. I believe it just busted her heart all up when my Dad died. Since I turned seventeen, I've been left alone to raise my brothers. It's the loneliest thing in the world trying to be in charge of parenting a bunch of kids when you are one. And there's loneliness in not being able to have any relationships because of all my responsibility. I changed. I had no friends, no girl. The only person who cared about me was my baseball coach. He let me bring my brothers with me on the bus and in the van to all my games."

I had the deepest admiration for young Robert. I asked him what had helped him through his hardship.

"My baseball coach," he said. "I realized that if one adult in your life knows you're lonely and reaches out to you, you're saved."✪

In a session I had with twenty kids in rural Atascadero, California, ten were underprivileged and the other ten were student council members from comfortable family backgrounds. The disadvantaged kids were dressed in cheap, saggy clothes. The student council members looked like they walked straight out of a Gap advertisement. I asked for the mixed session so that these two disparate groups could hear each other's viewpoints.

Early in the session, a sandy haired, scruffy looking boy named Billy rose from his seat. He exploded with anger as he told his story.

"My step-dad ran over my bike and destroyed it. It wasn't even in the driveway but over on the side. My bike is how I get to school. I live four miles away.

"That night when he got home, he came in my room and grabbed me and beat me till I couldn't hear anymore. I couldn't hear for four days. I've got to take it because my Mom and little sister live there, and he pays rent."

I was focused on Billy as he told his stirring story and didn't notice the rest of the group. Then I looked around. I saw the co-captain cheerleader, covered with ribbons and awards, dripping tears onto her desk. To take the attention off Billy, who had become so emotional, I asked the cheerleader if she was alright.

Through her tears, she said, "I used to get depressed when my Mom and Dad asked me to clean my room."

Everyone burst out with laughter, including Billy. We laughed for five minutes, bringing a welcome relief from the tension. As I looked at the kids before me, I saw a different light in everyone's eyes. Communication will do that. ✪

At Warren G. Harding Junior High in Philadelphia, teachers were stymied. Some of their students often walked out in the middle of classes because they had abnormally brief attention spans. Those kids would just wander the hallways and the schoolyard aimlessly. Teachers found the behavior frustrating, but they understood why it was happening. Many of the kids suffered from fetal cocaine syndrome. Their mothers were addicted to crack, and the result was children who can't keep their focus for any extended period of time. Unfortunately, children with fetal cocaine syndrome have a deficient ability to learn, and there's really nothing teachers can do about it. The principal, Mr. Gaffney, told me, "I used to have two or three kids like that. Now I have fifty."

One of them was a boy who I'll call Donny. Mr. Gaffney told me that Donny had seen some horrific violence; his mother was shot to death right in front of him. The poor boy had stopped talking because of it. I worked with Donny one entire week until finally I asked him if he ever spoke to anyone about the night he had seen his mother killed.

Donny looked at me with solemn eyes that had lost all of their tears long ago and said, "I don't want to, Big Mike. I never want to think about it. But sometimes my brain will just burp it up."

That's the greatest description of posttraumatic stress disorder that I've ever heard. Inadvertently, our brains will burp something up that we try with all of our willpower to suppress. It bubbles up and pops into our consciousness, forcing us to relive those memories we try to block out. Our societal dilemma is to figure out how to make breakthroughs to kids like Donny and those who suffer from similar problems. ✪

An African American boy named Flip was trying to explain to kids from the New Jersey suburbs what it was like to grow up in his inner-city neighborhood and how he was embittered towards white kids who didn't understand.

"My Dad was a highly decorated Marine [who fought in] Korea and all of his life he prided himself on being a member of the community. We were driving up the street and he beeped the horn at some kids who were in the middle of the street who wouldn't move out of the way. They were just standing around talking in the middle of the street. My Dad beeped the horn again.

"I said, 'Daddy please don't beep the horn. Those guys are G's.' And my Dad looked at me and said, 'G? What the hell is a G?' He didn't realize they were gangsters. They were maybe sixteen or seventeen, but they can be dangerous if you disrespect them. So after we passed around them, they yelled some stuff to us and my Dad told them to get out of the way. Then they shot into the back of our car three, four times. My Dad drove down away and we escaped. He sat behind the wheel and wept. He was ashamed because we lived in a neighborhood where somebody could take your life for just beeping the horn because they were in the way. It was the first time I saw my Dad cry.

"Another time, I was coming home from church in my suit and tie with one of my best friends and we were stopped at a red light. A crack head just walked over to the car and whipped a gun out and put it to my friend's head and clicked the hammer back and squeezed a round off. The crack head looked surprised because the gun didn't have any bullets in it. We were scared to death, so we sped off.

"That's the neighborhood I'm growing up in. That a man could take your life for nothing right after church. I want kids from the white suburbs to know that you can't understand what we're living with. You can't relate to what we live through and try to survive." ✪

I met Rondell and Geoffrey, twin African American boys, at a session in Richmond, California. Rondell was a kind, well-mannered gospel singer. Geoffrey was tough, cynical and angry. Rondell talked about their harrowing life.

"When I was twelve, my Grandmother got tired of it all. She turned the drug dealers in. Me and my brother had to sleep on a mattress inside the bathtub for protection. Inside the inside of the house, is what we called it. They shot her house up for turning in drug dealers and killed her. They brought in a foster mother for awhile for me and my brother, but the foster care woman didn't love us like our Grandmother did."

The boy put his head down to cry. I glanced at his twin brother, Geoffrey, who seemed pissed off that his life had been laid out on the table. The other kids in the session were overwhelmed with compassion for the twins and their tragic tale.

I looked across the room at their teacher and became quietly incensed. The teacher was sound asleep and hadn't heard one word the boy had said.

I tell teachers all the time, if you're burned out, get out. Teaching isn't manufacturing. You're not working at a factory making widgets. Those are lovely, wondrous spirits you're trying to inspire. Teachers should be like healers: First, do no harm. And indifference is harm.✪

The very first day after the tragedy at Columbine High School in Colorado, I met a group of students in Compton, California. One of the young men said this to me:

"Yo, Mr. Pritchard, I don't mean no disrespect for those kids that lost their lives, but I'll tell you something right now, man. We've had seven, eight people killed in this neighborhood in the past year, and we had nobody come down here for no safe school foundation or anything like that. We got no attention. We had nobody come down here for years. But let a couple of billionaire sons go off, and they got CBS News coming back from some war in the Middle East. Well, the real war is here in America."

Kids know the inequity in school systems, and it's the most urgent necessity for all of us to find a way to create equality in American education. ✪

Brentwood, California, is an upscale section of Greater Los Angeles located between Beverly Hills and the beaches at Santa Monica. Many of the children in the sun-soaked community come from affluent families; there is no 'bad part' of Brentwood. Yet those kids have issues, too.

I held a forum at a high school, and a teenage Madonna look-alike stood up before the group. She was petite yet sinewy. The tough girl confronted the entire class.

"You know what, you don't know me. You don't know anything about me. You judge me. You call me a slut. Some of you call me trailer court trash. Some of you call me the Madonna bitch. You all have a label for me. But none of you know my soul.

"So let's get it straight. I have a baby. I have a grandmother who I take care of. She has advanced Alzheimer's. The people I had been living with, my step-dad and my mom, are incapable of taking care of her. So I hire someone to take care of her while I work two jobs and take care of my baby. So excuse me if I don't have time to listen to your whining about how tough things are at home. Because I understand how tough things can get and I'm dealing with them every day.

"My grandmother is a loving person who deserves to be treated well. And my baby was a mistake but I'll never treat her as such, because she's taught me love. And I'm dealing with teachers at school who I know care about me deeply and want me to succeed, but I have to have that battle within me. I have to be able to say to myself, 'I want to succeed.'

"So excuse me if I don't listen to you moan and piss about life, 'cause I'm dealing with it already."

When she sat down, an enormous young man in the group spoke to the girl. In a quavering voice, he said, "Uh, I just want to apologize to you. I'm so sorry. I'm ashamed of myself for the way I treated you. I called you every one of those names, and I laughed when others called you those names. And I didn't know anything about you.

I'm truly ashamed of myself, because I have a hard life and I know what that's like. I don't expect you to be my friend, but I want you to know that I'll never treat you like that again."

I told the kids that what they said was awesome. That was the work that needs to get done. It's all about understanding one another.

Later, a 30-year teacher said to me, "You'll never know how important it was to see the block of ice melt from around that girl's heart." ✪

Fifteen-year-old Maria sat quietly among her fellow students. She wore dirty tennis shoes and blue jeans that were torn at the knees. Her hair was pulled back tightly. I sensed that she wanted to speak, but she was too shy to address the gathering.

My friend Buterez, a San Antonio D.A.R.E. police officer, attended the session with me. He stood off to one side while I faced the kids.

A Hispanic boy held the floor, talking about how another student hit him in the back of the head every time he bent over to open his locker. I asked him how that made him feel.

"It doesn't bother me."

"Why not?" I asked. "Are you Superman?"

That brought a wry grin to his face. "I know that soon I'm going to get a really good job at my uncle's auto body shop, and I'm going to be making good money, and I'm going to get a really nice car. I know the kid who hits me everyday acts all tough, but he's flunking out of school, and he's got nobody."

"Well, I'm proud of you, Manuel," I said. "You get the big picture. Anybody else?"

Maria sat low in her seat and timidly raised her tiny hand. When I called on her, she delivered her tale with heartbreaking honesty.

"It's hard for me at school because the kids call me Stinky. They make fun of the way I dress. I saved twelve bucks from doing chores for people, and my mother said she would match it with another twelve bucks so I could get a new pair of jeans at the Wal-Mart. That same day, the bills came, and my Mom told me she couldn't help after all."

Maria sobbed loudly, and her fellow students were struck silent by her pain. Another girl put her arm around Maria for comfort.

Often, we judge people by their appearances when we don't know the facts about them. I'm sure those kids wouldn't have called her Stinky had they only known her family's dire financial straits. Most kids will feel empathy or apologize when made to see how their actions have affected someone else.

I heard my friend Buterez, the police officer, sniffling. He's a big, proud Mexican-American who sees pain and brutality routinely in his job, things that harden a man. Yet after hearing Maria speak to her class, I watched Buterez cry just as hard as that shy little girl. Sometimes when you see a child who carries that much pain, you can't escape it. You can only feel it. And maybe Buterez was reflecting on his own impoverished childhood.

Rather than going to a restaurant for a fancy meal with the members of the local board as we had planned, I convinced Buterez that we should help Maria's family instead. That night, he and I took groceries and blue jeans to their home.

The next day, I saw shy Maria but she avoided eye contact with me. Her brother approached me, though, wearing a Tasmanian Devil T-shirt and wearing thick eyeglasses that looked like the bottoms of Coca Cola bottles.

He told me, "My Mom says that you are building it brick by brick."

"What am I building brick by brick?"

"Your mansion in heaven."

That overwhelmed me. Tears sprang from my eyes.

"Are you crying?" the boy asked.

"Yeah, sometimes people cry," I said.

"Are you sad?"

"No, you made me feel good about who I am."

"Are you sure you're not sad?"

"Why do you suppose someone might cry when they're happy?" I asked.

The little seven-year-old boy looked up at me and said, "Maybe their heart fills up and then their eyes spill over."

I don't think I've ever heard a poet so eloquently describe the process of brimming with love and joy. ✪

"There are nine categories of angels in the world. The greatest of these are the seraphim and the cherubim. The seraphim have all love, and the cherubim have all knowledge. But you'll notice that the seraphim are always closest to the throne, because throughout all time love has been more important than knowledge. How could we ever forget that?"

- Annie Dillard

Kids At Risk Are Kids With Potential

"To be yourself, in a world that tries, night and day,
to make you just like everybody else –
is to fight the greatest battle there ever is to fight..."
e.e cummings

There's a term in education that drives me crazy – at-risk kids. This indicates children with emotional instability, drug or alcohol abuse in their families, or disadvantages due to poverty. Generally speaking, these kids are supposedly at risk of behaving badly and/or being unable to meet minimum requirements expected of them in school, and hence in society. That's how the education system looks at them. It's a negative connotation.

In my opinion, the term should be 'a child with potential.' There are incredible, heartfelt possibilities in all of these kids. Besides, a child doesn't have to be financially disadvantaged to be at risk of bad behavior. Here's what I mean.

I spoke with a public research interest group at an Ivy League college, and I confronted the young men and women about inappropriate public behavior. Some students were acting maliciously towards rival basketball players during Final Four tournament games. While sitting in the stands, they held up diapers to taunt one opposing player who had an illegitimate baby. Another player, who had a father in prison, was ridiculed with the chant, "Where's your daddy now? Where's your daddy now?" Another basketball player with a marijuana conviction was similarly taunted. The students were trying to disturb the players so they'd miss foul shots or misplay the ball. I told the college students that such vicious behavior was absolutely reprehensible, especially from privileged men and women attending a $35,000-per-year private school. It was shameful.

An argument erupted in which the twenty-year-olds made mean-spirited and inappropriate comments about me to my face. They accused me of being a politically correct blowhard and a bitter old man who had no right to lecture them.

Then a black woman, a college junior, stood up in the back of the room and spoke. "When you came in here, I thought you were going to be one of those politically correct people, but now I know that you're not. I understand where you're coming from. You're just a big fat old dad like my dad. My daddy's a mailman. I have a scholarship here 'cause of my grades and my ability at literature and poetry.

"So here's the deal. I can't stand to be in this school at lunchtime. 'Cause when you go to the girl's bathroom, a lot of these girls, whose moms and dads are spending truckloads of money to bring them here, are purging their lunches into the sink. They go together to get their gag responses up. And the school knows about it because they've gotta replace those pipes because of the acid washing the pipes away. Those girls are sick. And the worst part is, I got children starving to death in my neighborhood [back home] while these girls puke their good lunches into that sink. Makes me ill."

Then she sat down. There was a stone silence in the room. A dozen of the young ladies in attendance, girls in leadership positions, hung their heads in shame, signifying to anyone who has ever been a probation officer or a detective that you're guilty.

So, the point is, who's really 'at risk?' Is it the kid from dire financial circumstances who strives to do the right thing? Or is it the rich kid who tries to be perfect yet acts inappropriately in public? Maybe the kid who's really 'at risk' grew up under a money tree, wears the finest clothes, gets the best grades, attends the ideal school, and lives his or her life entirely focused on external validations. By contrast, I've met many kids who've been labeled 'at risk' who are soul-searchers and who deal with truly devastating hardships as best they can. They have more positive character traits than some Ivy Leaguers I've met. ✪

I knew a cynical African-American teen named Robin who used to say things like, "It wouldn't be raining outside if I were white." "That light would have turned green by now if I was white." Sure, he was joking, but there was always anger behind it. His mother, a respected nurse, asked me to speak to him about his cynicism.

He told me that he'd never be able to find a decent job because he was a black kid who went to a disrespected school. But I argued that he attended the same high school as actor Danny Glover. Robin wasn't impressed. I told him to stop wallowing in self-pity about his life.

Then I made him come with me to the recreation center for the handicapped. He was with me all day long. I told Robin not to talk, but just to observe. He watched me change urine bags and wiped bottoms and feed a young person with cerebral palsy. I had to catch the food as it was regurgitated. Robin had to walk away three times because he was sickened by what he saw.

When we left, I asked if he had anything to say.

He said, "Yeah. I do. I'm ashamed of myself. Because I complained. And when I saw that, I knew I shouldn't."

That eight-hour day changed Robin's life, as I suspected it would. As Martin Luther King, Jr. said, "We can all be great because we can all serve. All we need is a heart full of grace." ✪

Stereotypically, Samoan kids are huge. That's not always fact, of course, but many stereotypes are based on common traits. Most of the Samoans I've met aren't insulted by the generality, because more often than not it's true.

Eddie was a seventeen-year-old Samoan, and he completely fit the stereotype. He was 300 pounds of solid muscle. His arms were massive, like he was carrying tree trunks up his sleeves. His no-neck head, on which he always wore a hair net, was like a boulder with eyes. When I had to take him into custody at San Francisco's Juvenile Hall, he was so broad that he had to walk into the cell sideways.

Despite the menacing depiction, Samoans are the gentlest, sweetest kids in the world. However, some of the teens I've met could be troublesome, too. Out on the street with a head full of liquor and drugs, they posed a tremendous challenge to law enforcement.

I brought Eddie into Juvenile Hall because he tore an antenna off a police car.

"I didn't know it was illegal, Big Mike," he told me.

"What? You didn't know it was illegal to tear an antenna off a cop car?"

"Yeah."

I laughed and said, " Ignorance is no excuse for the law."

"Yeah but it's better than no alibi at all" said Eddie.

He didn't fool me. I knew Eddie was smarter than that. He was a good kid who attended church on Sunday with his Mom. "It says here you struck an officer."

"I didn't hit nobody. The cop got scared of me and started spraying mace in my face. I leaned my head back and took all the mace in my mouth and gargled it. Then I spit it on the ground and said, 'Now, what are you going to do, Brother?' And the cop looked at me and said, 'I think I'm going to leave if you let me.' You see, Big Mike, I can't control myself when I get drunk, man. I don't even remember. But I don't mean to hurt nobody."

I got Eddie to commit to going to AA meetings, and he eventually cleaned himself up. No more spitting out mace. Today, he's doing well and he even sings in the church choir.

Some kids' problems are as large and heavy as an iceberg. But give them enough sunshine and that iceberg will melt. ✪

I'm haunted by the sad tale of Vaughn, a teenager from New Orleans, Louisiana.

Mr. Wilton, the principal of the school that Vaughn attended, asked if I could speak to the young man alone. The teachers and school staff were frightened of him. No one knew what to do with Vaughn. Mr. Wilton told me that the boy was seen in his neighborhood carrying a .32 automatic. Vaughn's mother was a former New Orleans police officer who was fired from her position on the force. She claimed that her son was the cause of her dismissal because Vaughn had gone through the neighborhood threatening to kill people.

I agreed to speak to the boy. Mr. Wilton arranged for us to meet in a private school room.

When Vaughn swaggered in, he reeked of attitude.

"I want to go to an all black school," he promptly told me.

"Why?"

"Because I hate white people."

"We all have to live on the streets together," I told him.

"I don't want to live on no street with no white ass motherfucker. I will shoot them down. I can't control myself."

I asked Vaughn where he got the gun.

"It was my Mother's."

"Your Mother says it was your attitude that got her fired from the police department."

"It wasn't me, it was her damn boyfriend! He was beating on her and she won't do anything. Now, she won't leave the son of a bitch 'cause she ain't got no job."

Sensing a familiar pattern, I asked, "Has your mother's boyfriend hurt you, too, Vaughn?"

His eyes welled up with tears. Suddenly, his braggadocio was replaced with heartrending silence.

The signs were fairly clear to me. I knew that the amount of hate that the boy harbored was probably brought on by physical and sexual assault. Vaughn couldn't look at me when I tried to console him, even though I insisted.

"You don't have to say anything if you don't want to," I said.

His silence spoke volumes.

Mr. Wilton was a very spiritual man. At last, he understood the cause of his student's rage. He took pity on the boy. Vaughn was only thirteen.

There's no lonelier existence for a child than to be abused and turned into an angry monster. But it doesn't help one iota for that child to be labeled 'at-risk' and then dismissed as if he were someone else's problem. ✪

When I was inducted into my high school's Hall of Fame, a nun approached me before I gave my acceptance speech. She begged me not to mention my high school indiscretions. I had to laugh. Naturally, I mentioned all of that within the first five seconds. I began my speech by saying, "I'm absolutely sure that I'm the first person inducted into this Hall of Fame who graduated with eleven suspensions and a straight D average."

But here's what no one knew when I was in high school. My father was dying of cancer at that time. He had been fired from his job.

We had no money. My Mom was a Catholic teacher at St. Dismus grade school, and she was ashamed of the fact I was a poor student. My brothers were good students, but I wasn't. My problem was that I had no ability to focus, because I was interested in everything. Everything! And when I graduated from high school, I learned that I have a photographic memory. That completely surprised my mother. She often badgered me with the line, "Well, if you can remember every stupid joke there is and every line of every song and every line of dialogue from every stupid TV show, then why can't you remember your lessons?"

I can recall attending an algebra class when I was young at which the teacher turned to me and said, "You are an idiot. You will always be an idiot. You'll never be able to do anything because you are an idiot."

Naturally, the entire class stared at me. That left an indelible psychological scar.

Another episode that scarred me was when my father was dying of cancer. In the middle of a class, a voice came of the public address system.

"Michael Pritchard, please come to the office for a talk to the financial people about your late tuition."

The adult on the intercom specifically stated why I was being called to the carpet. It wasn't anything I had done: It was an insult to my family, to my Dad, to my Mom. I had to rise from my seat and walk past all of my classmates who mocked me with fake cries of pity. (Kids can be sick and cruel, can't they?) It was the longest walk I ever took through the school. But I survived it.

There was no name for it back then, but in today's education system a child like me with poor grades and financial instability at home would be labeled at-risk. Clearly, though, I was a child with potential. No one looked beyond my test scores to unearth the root cause of my difficulties. Sure, I turned out alright, if I may say so myself, but not every kid in similar circumstances does. Every single child, regardless of plight, deserves to have an adult reach out to them and help find the causes of his or her strife. Then and only then can a child be given the fair opportunity to achieve his or her potential. ✪

Sitting in a sweat tent is a traditional Native American ritual. It's exactly what it sounds like. Men sit together in a heated tent or a lodge and sweat. It's similar to a Turkish bath except that sage and other herbs are used to purify the air for health benefits. The idea is simple; perspiring cleanses you physically and spiritually.

I was invited to a Wyoming reservation where there was a rash of child suicides. It was a sad time for those Native American kids, and I was a bit lost about how to reach them.

After meeting with the kids, an Arapaho tribal elder, the shaman, invited me to sit with him in the sweat tent. Huge drops of perspiration cascaded off of me. I was like a human tropical rainstorm. The heat was so intense that I found it hard to catch my breath. But the 80-year-old shaman beside me seemed unfazed.

"You have met with the children today," the old man said to me. "What did you find out?"

I said, "In all honesty, I was hoping you could offer me some guidance."

The shaman spoke in a low, sad voice. "I know why they are killing themselves."

"Why?" I asked.

"Satellite dishes."

I was skeptical. "Satellite dishes?"

"They see everything they can't have," he said, "everything they don't own, everything they want to be but are not, everything they want to wear but don't have, and everywhere they want to go but aren't going. They feel that the land is not theirs anymore. They don't feel the land as we did when we were young. They all want something else away from here. It is hard for me as a leader because this is our sacred land. Yet we are in the land of the hopeless. I believe it is hopeless for them." He wiped sweat from his forehead. "But you have spoken to the children and listened to them with your heart. So please tell me what you think."

With due respect and humility, I chuckled and replied, "Well, sir, can I say, first of all, that I think you're a really shitty holy man? Because what kind of holy man has no hope?"

The two of us roared with laughter. He leaned back and let out a cackle that probably cleansed his soul as well, if not better than, all that perspiring.

When we came out of the tent later, the shaman's daughter, who had heard our laughter, said, "Well, you two certainly had a good time."

The shaman chuckled and said, "Yeah, and no whiskey, either. Heh, heh."

Before I left, I said seriously, "The children can't look outside for the answers. Your job is to lead them inside to the answers." I tapped my chest as I spoke.

The elderly man pointed at me and nodded in total understanding. He realized how he had been remiss as a leader. Then he said, "Sometimes when we are hurting, we forget which way the sun goes down." ✪

Girl Talk

"You call me a bitch like that's a bad thing."
Bumper sticker on a car

Teen girls just reaching puberty can be extremely cruel and create incredible pain in each other's lives. How society can accept this as a right of passage for young girls is beyond my comprehension. Some argue that cruelty is normal in that age group. Yet it shouldn't be. And such behavior shouldn't go unnoticed. Because girls grow up to carry relationship scars for a lifetime. Junior high school is the time when they learn to relate to people. Correcting cruelty must begin then or they'll suffer for it down the road.

I asked a group of Bronx schoolgirls how it made them feel to be called bitch all the time. A girl responded, "If they want to call me a bitch because I say I'm not going to get in a car with a drunk, I'm not going to go shoplift with you guys, I am not going to go out and party around a bunch of potheads who make my streets unsafe, and I am not going to stand around and disrespect somebody's home and knock stuff over in it and then escape before the parents get home because you think it's funny…That's not who I am. If that makes me a bitch, then so be it, I'm a bitch."

Then a tough Puerto Rican girl said, "I have friends who aren't loyal to a fault, but are faithful to a fault."

Confused, I asked what was the difference between being loyal and faithful.

She said, "Loyal people can sometimes be stupid. They can go with you when you're going to do the wrong thing. They can go with you when you're going to go and get into a fight. You're going to get hurt and they're going to get hurt. They just want to do it because they got your back. But faithful people are the people that know that there is something inside you worth saving and to be your friend. And to protect you, not just from the outside world but also from you making bad choices." ✪

I posed the same question to girls at a high school in Tallahasee, Florida. A girl with long blonde hair said, "My mom is always calling her friends a bitch, so I started using it all the time. I thought I was really popular and all, and then I heard this other girl when I passed her in the hall call me a bitch. Then I got pissed off and yelled back really loud, 'Bitch!' And then she yelled back at me, 'Bigger bitch!' And then I yelled back, 'Bigger bitch than me!' And then everybody in the hall started laughing at us.

"So I went to class thinking about how I looked so foolish and how I was always using that word. So I asked my best friend, 'Am I a bitch?' And she wouldn't answer. Probably scared I would call her a bitch. I said, 'You don't have to be nice to me to be my friend, you just have to be real. Tell me the truth.' And she said, 'Well, you're not a bitch but...'

"Then I knew I was one."

One girl told me that bitch is an acronym for Babe In Total Control of Herself. That's a clever way of turning a negative into a positive, but that's obviously not the intent when someone calls a girl a bitch.

Words can be arrows on our character. Teach a kid to build a spiritual wall against them. Don't shoot back the arrows that are shot at you. ✪

In 1979, I appeared on television performing stand-up comedy. A San Francisco woman named Eva saw me on TV and called Catholic Charities. She asked if they could arrange for me to help her and her children. "My husband beats me," she said.

On hearing this, I formulated a plan to take Eva and her children from the house where they lived and place them in a shelter. Before going to get the family, I called my friend Bernie Shaw, a sergeant in Community Affairs. I explained that I was going to take the family to Casa de las Madres, a well-known shelter, and asked if the battered woman's husband had any prior convictions. I was told that he didn't and that "it's all clear." So I drove to the woman's house.

Shortly after that call, Bernie's computer printer started spitting out information to the contrary – the batterer had a long criminal record that included assault, battery, vehicular manslaughter, and eight years served for armed robbery. Bernie was shocked. He tried to reach me with the information, but it was too late. I was already on my way to get Eva and her kids. Realizing that I was probably headed into a dangerous situation, Bernie sprang into action.

I parked my car on Monterey Boulevard and walked one block to Eva's home, oblivious that I was going into harm's way. Suddenly, six police SWAT team vehicles roared along the street. I stopped to see what the parade of cop cars was all about. Then all six cruisers pulled up next to me!

SWAT officers leapt from the vehicles and instructed me to move off to safety. A female officer wearing protective yellow shooting glasses racked her automatic weapon. Officers Mahoney and Murphy approached me.

"Oh, no, not my guy," I said in amazement. They told me he was wanted and extremely dangerous.

The lead officers kicked in the door and took the suspect into custody. I went in moments later when it was clear. I called out for Eva. No response. But what I saw in their living room stunned me.

A little black boy, no more than three years old, sat in front of the television set trembling. He wouldn't take his eyes off of the screen. Clearly, he was trying to pretend that the incident with the police hadn't occurred. Yet he was frightened to death. I later learned that his name was Devon.

I took the boy to my car where I left him in the care of a woman from the shelter. Then I went inside the house and found an infant, changed its diaper, and took the baby to the social worker, too. Then I went back into the house to search for Eva. I searched throughout the house and finally found her hiding in an ironing board closet, her body compressed tightly into the tiny space as if she were trying to blend into the wall. I gently helped her out of the closet. She had choke marks all around her neck, a tooth knocked out, a black eye, and bruises all over her body.

She cried and shouted at me, "You son of a bitch! You ruined our Christmas!"

That left me speechless.

"I wanted you to help him get a job!" she cried.

There's a cliché among social workers who deal with battered woman. Too often the victims will say of their husbands or boy-friends, 'He may be a bastard, but he's my bastard, and he's the only bastard who'll take care of me.' That clearly applied to misguided Eva.

I took Eva and her kids to Casa de las Madres where they were given the opportunity to start anew. Unfortunately, Eva's pathetic life continued to spiral downward. She eventually died of AIDS. Her children were placed into the foster care system, and both are doing very well today.

I checked in on Devon, Eva's eldest son, when he was fourteen. He had grown up with a wonderful new family in a Bay Area city. His adopted mother asked if Devon knew who I was. It had been over ten years since I took him from that horrible situation, and he was only a little boy at the time. But he nodded his head with imme-diate recognition. Nothing more needed to be said.

I knew his life had changed for the better when I saw his bed-room, which is every kid's private space and place of identity. I no-ticed that he owned all of the things that any kid would want, that he was surrounded by love, and that he was leading a happy life. ✪

Girls often tell me that while boys fight and punch and wrestle one another, girls call each other names and give one another eating disorders. That's the unfortunate truth wherever I go, especially among girls from upper middle class and wealthy families. It's unsettling to hear prepubescent teenage girls sit together and discuss their weight. This is the biggest problem I see with today's girls; they're consumed by external validations. They buy all the magazines and see what they're supposed to look like, what they're supposed to wear, what make-up they need to apply, what fashion is in style and what's 'so last year,' and so on. It's taken to such extremes that it's frightening.

A pudgy twelve-year-old at a California middle school stood up during one of my sessions. The eighth grader wept as she told the entire school full of children her shocking story. "My Mom spent two thousand dollars to send me to summer camp, and then (another student's) mother called my Mom and told her, 'Your daughter shouldn't go to this camp. Believe me. She shouldn't be seen in a swimming suit.'"

That moment was quite possibly the most painful I'd ever witnessed. That an adult, believing she was doing a favor, could unconsciously pour pain on a child's spirit still fills me with anger. All of us have an obligation to intervene against thoughtless adults and give them a clue. ✪

I spoke to two girls who had a terrible rivalry. They never fought physically, but theirs was a war of words. "We used to be friends," one of the girls told me, "but now we spend all of our time seeing who can send to other one home crying that day."

I said, "Do you realize how sick that sounds?"

The girl replied, "Who cares? I won today." ✪

At a completely different school, I met a teenager who I'll call Rene. I heard her tell a classmate, "You shouldn't come to school at all unless you find someone to give you fashion tips." Rene looked and spoke as seriously as if she were giving advice to someone who was slowly killing herself by smoking cigarettes.

A boy stood up in defense of the insulted girl and said, "Who made you the queen of fashion?"

Rene's reply was, "At least I have subscriptions to magazines so that I know what goes with what."

I asked Rene if she realized how badly she had insulted her fellow classmate.

Her earnest response was, "Hey, I'm just trying to wake her up."

"No, you hurt the girl's feelings," I insisted. Then I turned to the insulted girl, who was teary-eyed, and said, "Please tell Rene that."

In a weak, quavering voice, the girl said, "You hurt my feelings."

Rene didn't waver, however. "Better to have your feelings hurt now than when you get into college and can't find a man."

That attitude was both laughable and sickening. It's another example of external validation in our kids; the almost archaic idea that clothes attract men. Rene bought into that erroneous philosophy that you are what you wear. ✪

I met a woman who gave a speech to kids about her personal hell with an eating disorder when she was young. Her aim was to scare the girls into awareness, and her words deeply affected me. The woman admitted to being so mentally disturbed by her problem as a girl that she was actually grateful when she contracted herpes around her mouth because it kept her from eating. That's how sick some of these girls can get! Grateful for herpes of the mouth!

This is the message that all kids need to hear. You can become deranged by your external validations. When sensitive people hear others talk about their weight, their noses, their ears, their hair, they run off to get it all 'repaired.' Think of the piles of money women spend on liposuction and cosmetic surgery. Yet that sense of beauty that must come from within. People who go under the knife to improve their looks don't deserve blame; if it gives them satisfaction, that's okay. But the best cosmetic of all is a happy life. That's what makes you beautiful. ✪

I like to tell a story to many of the young girls I meet. It comes from a book by Sara Halprin titled *Look At My Ugly Face: Myths and Musings on Beauty and Other Perilous Obsessions with Women's Appearance* (Viking Press, 1995).

King Arthur faced Sir Grommet on the field of battle, and the combatant was prepared to take the king's head. But Grommet said, "If you can tell me what women most want, I will spare your life." In self-preservation, Arthur naturally agreed.

He traveled through the land with his best friend, Sir Gawain, in search of the answer. He visited monasteries and wise men and magi and all of the seats of knowledge. But the answers he received were unsatisfactory.

Finally, Sir Grommet's sister, Lady Ragsdale, an old maid who was considered the ugliest woman in history, approached Arthur. Her eyes were like dead leaves and her face was like tree bark. No one would marry her. She professed to know what women want, and she was prepared to tell Arthur on one condition. She told the king, "If you will convince Sir Gawain to marry me, I will give you the answer you seek."

"I cannot ask Gawain to do that," Arthur said, "because he would comply merely out of fealty to his king."

True to form, when Gawain heard of the proposition, he agreed to marry Lady Ragsdale on the spot. On the day of their wedding, Lady Ragsdale told her man, "I can either be beautiful during the day or during the evening, but you must choose."

Gawain said, "I will not choose. You must choose for yourself. It makes no difference because you're always beautiful to me."

And with that, the spell that she had been under was broken. Lady Ragsdale was transformed from a hag into one of the loveliest women in the land because Gawain helped her find her inner beauty. He had also given Lady Ragsdale her heart's desire – free will.

When Arthur met Sir Grommet on the field of battle a second time, Grommet raised his sword to behead the king. He posed the question, "What do women want most?"

And Arthur replied, "Free will."

Sir Grommet dropped his weapon. It was the correct answer, and he knew his own sister had betrayed him. Grommet then wandered out into the forest and fell on his sword.

The moral of the story: Free will transforms any woman into a rare beauty. ✪

The Poverty of Loneliness

*The most terrible poverty is loneliness
and the feeling of being unloved.
Mother Teresa*

When I was young, my Dad would stand on the front porch of our Missouri home and whistle for his sons. It was a distinctively loud and clear whistle, like that of a cowboy rounding up his herd. When we heard that sound, my brothers and I would stampede toward the house. We all knew it was the signal for dinner.

My Mom's cooking never won any culinary awards, to put it kindly. We blamed it on her Irish heritage. But we were big boys with bottomless pits for stomachs, so we ate her bland meals anyway.

My Grandfather, in his Irish brogue, would comment on Mom's cooking.

"I've seen cows that recovered from worse than this."

He'd point to the meat and say, "Look, boys, you can still see the whip marks from the jockey."

Despite Mom's flavorless cooking, my brothers and I always raced home whenever we heard Dad's unmistakable whistle.

One day, I walked out of our house and found a boy sitting on our front porch. I recognized him from our neighborhood, but I didn't understand why he was sitting alone on our steps. A tear slithered down his cheek. I asked him why he was crying.

"Did my brothers say something mean to you?"

"No."

"Did someone pick on you?"

"No."

"Are you hurt?"

"No."

"Then why are you crying?"

"I don't have anybody to whistle me home."

Reaching out to the lonely child blesses a human being deeply. Acknowledge children's pain, their isolation, and their sadness. Just lend them an ear. That connection can transform a spirit and bring it back to life. ✪

I performed one afternoon for kids at a group home in California, and a boy approached me after the show. We'll call him Peter. He was a short, skinny eight-year-old.

"Can I speak to you in private?" Peter asked.

I assumed that he had something important to tell me, so I gladly obliged him. We walked to the back of the room away from everyone else and sat in chairs next to each other. Even sitting, I towered over the little boy.

I asked if everything was okay for him at the group home.

"Yeah," he said. "My friends call me Pee Wee and Squirt or whatever, but I know they like me 'cause they bought me a Walkman." His short legs couldn't reach the floor, so he happily kicked them in the air.

I asked about school.

"I'm getting great grades. I'm in third grade and I'm getting A's and B's."

I asked if he liked Father Dave, the group home's organizer.

"Yeah, he's my buddy. He gives me rides on the tractor."

We discussed other pleasant yet mundane topics for several minutes until I had exhausted all my questions of what I thought he might want to share with me. Since my subtle promptings failed, I just came out with it.

"Peter, what did you want to talk about?"

"Oh, no, I just wanted to *be* with you." he explained.

Peter was starved for fatherly attention, and he was clever enough to single me out. The lonely boy wanted nothing more than to spend the rest of the day just being with me.

I understood what he meant. When I was young, my Grandfather would drink a couple of shots of bourbon and then pass out in his favorite chair. His cigar stunk up the room as he dozed. I'd sit at his side just to be with him, but I would never wake him up. I appreciated Grandpa because he was my link to the past. Okay, maybe I'd sneak a puff of his White Owl cigar now and then, but that wasn't why I sat next to him. Sometimes you just want to be with people. ✪

My three older brothers were gigantic boys. They were built like vending machines with heads. And all three were athletes. One was a great track star, one a football quarterback, and the other was a killer in rugby. I didn't run well, I was too uncoordinated to throw a ball, and I didn't want to compete. I just didn't get it. What was the point of all of that running and hitting and chasing a ball?

My brothers constantly tormented me to join them in sports. They teased me mercilessly until I caved in. They said things like, "Mom dusts the furniture harder than you can hit me."

Or they'd say, "You run like some kind of tropical bird."

The worst insult of all was, "You throw like a girl!"

My brothers had a great time making fun of me. Sure, it hurt, but I got used to it. They'd fire off the insults, but I learned to let them roll off my back. I knew that I was different from my brothers.

As a result, I spent a lot of time alone watching television. I would escape to the basement where I lived in darkness, except for the glow of my TV set. My world was inside that little box. That box didn't make fun of me. It didn't torment me. I could control that box.

In every session, I see kids like me who escape to a box. For some, their safe world is in a computer. For some, it's television. For others, it's books. The worst cases, however, are the kids who escape to the box in their very own mind.

Often, these are the kids who turn to drugs for escapism. The more they frequent their private worlds, the more they pull away from normal social activities. The more they isolate themselves, the more depressed they become. And when these kids feel that they're all alone with their problems, suicide and violence can occur. ✪

During a meeting with a group of high school students in Novato, California, I asked if any of them knew the experience of being alone.

One handsome, bright-eyed young man answered.

"When I was a freshman, I looked different. I wasn't into sports at all. I liked to read a lot. I was really into music and art. I just did what I wanted to do, not what everybody else wanted me to do. People would call me names and tease me all the time."

I asked if he was called names, and if so, what were they.

"Faggot, loser, retard, weirdo. I used to have a Mohawk. I guess I had it because my Father was always telling me I was no good. I wasn't smart enough. I was never going to be anything. One night, these guys jumped me and beat me up just because of the way I was dressed."

"Were you angry?" I asked.

"Not necessarily angry at one person," he said. "I was just disappointed at the world. In my freshman year, I hung around with this kid who looked different, like me. But this guy kept talking about killing himself. He never told me why. He just kept talking about it. The other kids at school made fun of him because he was different, so he just sat in his room a lot and listened to music.

"One day, he got his father's gun and shot himself. He died. I couldn't believe it. And I thought, 'How could I have helped my friend who was so alone?' I didn't even see it coming. I mean, he talked about it, but I just thought it was talk. It really affected me.

"I joined the peer-counseling group at school and shaved my Mohawk off. I mean, it was cool and all. Now, I've learned that my friend was showing signs that he felt really alone. I guess, maybe, I could have helped him better. But his life has changed me for the rest of mine." ✪

I sat in an exquisite library inside a private school in Massachusetts surrounded by teens whose parents had paid a small fortune for them to attend. They were no different from teens anywhere else; some were neat, some were grubby, a few were jocks, many were ordinary in every regard. I saw one common trait, though. Most of them had sad expressions. I had been brought in because of an alarming increase in drug use on campus.

Try as I might to connect to the kids, I felt they were aloof and disinterested. At first, I attributed this to the fact that most of the teens came from wealthy backgrounds and were bored with everything. Then I sensed a deeper problem. They were listening to me but appeared to be afraid to talk.

Jason was a skinny boy with dyed-blonde hair and several piercings in his ears. He opened up and admitted that he used drugs because he was often all alone.

"Isn't there anybody you can talk to?" I asked.

"No," he answered as he pulled his legs up close to his chest.

"What about your Mom or Dad?"

"No way. They're never home."

"Somebody? A counselor? A relative?"

"I have a therapist," he admitted.

"That's good. Have you talked to your therapist about being alone?"

That caused an explosion of laughter from the group, which completely surprised me. My bewildered expression surely gave away the fact that I didn't get the joke, whatever it was.

Lydia, a girl dressed head-to-toe in black with matching black nail polish, offered me the explanation. "Mr. Pritchard, everyone here has a therapist."

"Everybody ? All sixteen of you?" I asked incredulously. "Well, can't any of you talk to your therapists?"

"No way," Lydia said, "I consider my therapist a paid informant for my Dad."

I felt a cold chill run down my back for those pitiable children. I wanted to give them all hugs. Instead, I gave them the assurance that I would tell no one what was said between us so long as they were honest about their feelings.

I asked Jason again how he felt when he was alone.

"It makes me feel sick."

"What's the loneliest moment in your life?" I asked

"I think..." He looked at a few of the other students and reconsidered.

I prodded to speak up, to be the first in the group.

Jason fought back the tears. "I think when I came home after three months away at school and my parents left me a note saying they were out and wouldn't be back till late. I know it sounds stupid."

I assured him that it wasn't. "Everybody deserves to be wanted," I said. "Knowing that somebody cares is the richest feeling in the world."

Jason put his head down as tears dripped on his baggy pants. There was a deep, painful silence in the room.

A thin boy who was crouched down in the back of the group snickered. I turned my attention to him. "Charles, are you laughing at Jason's pain?"

No answer.

"I think Jason's the bravest person in this room," I continued. "I would hope you're not that cynical to laugh when somebody is hurt. Because you know what that tells me, Charles? You hurt more than Jason but you're just afraid to admit it. A brave person faces his fear but a coward hides it with cynicism."

Lydia let out a big breath. "He's got you there, Chucky!"

I let her have the floor.

"Yeah, Mr. Pritchard, Charles is the ring leader of tormented cynicism around here. He's called me fat and a freak since I can remember. But you know what, you're right. I don't think I've ever seen Charles go home to visit his parents."

Before Charles even had a chance to respond, another girl, Jocelyn, told her story of being alone whenever her parents traveled. Eventually, the other kids opened up and admitted similar stories. Hearing the sad admissions of loneliness left them all feeling more in touch to one another's pain.

Some people would refer to those children as privileged. But it's no privilege to suffer loneliness. It's no privilege to be unsure if your parents truly care for you. And it's no privilege to be afraid to speak out about it. ✪

I visited a high school in Washington, DC, that seemed to be split in two. Half of the students came from very poor inner city homes, mostly African Americans. The other half were racially diverse rich kids from Washington's elite families. Everyone, strangely enough, dressed the same. But it was their attitudes more than anything that divided the kids.

When I met with a group of these teens, we listened to one of the boys talk about being a "latch key kid." Let's call him Jeffrey. He complained that he was always alone.

I asked him, "If you're a latch key kid, can't you have friends over if you get lonely?"

He said, "No, I'm too ashamed."

"Do you live in a tough neighborhood?" I asked.

"I live in a thirty-eight room mansion."

That surprised me. I asked what the problem was.

"Well, I come home and there's a microwave meal in the oven from the housekeeper. I eat that and then I go upstairs to watch big screen TV in my bedroom or do my homework. Every night, I pray that my alcoholic socialite parents will get home alive because they drink and drive too much. You see, I'm adopted. I think my parents adopted me because I was an acquisition. Their friends had kids, so why shouldn't they? But they just don't have any relationship with me. They buy me all kinds of stuff but they don't really care about me."

I asked Jeffrey what was stopping him from having friends over if he was lonely.

"I'm ashamed that they might come over to my house and think that I have everything. That I'm spoiled. But at least they get to go home and somebody's there."

That was followed by a long, sad silence. None of the other kids in the room knew what to say. Then a plump African American girl reached over and patted the lonely boy on the back.

"You poor, poor baby," she said. "You need to come over to my house and let my Mama make you some cookies."

The group of kids howled with laughter. But the compassion of that one girl from poorer circumstances reaching out to the privileged boy from a mansion was priceless. It helped me realize the power of letting kids open up and talk amongst one another. We can help kids deal with loneliness by listening to their grief and feeling their pain. ✪

A comedian I knew needed drug rehabilitation, and I helped him through it. He had terribly low self-esteem and was painfully self-critical. I told him, "You remind me of a guy who would never kick a man when he was down, unless that man was you."

I often tell people that when they psychologically beat themselves up they shouldn't expect me to sit by and allow them to do that. Just as you wouldn't stand back and watch child abuse, you shouldn't permit a friend to verbally abuse himself or herself. Ask your friends to not speak about themselves so disparagingly. When you do, your friends are sure to be grateful.

Self-esteem is an important trait. We shouldn't be hard on ourselves. Nobody's perfect. I asked an eleven-year-old in North Carolina, "Do you think you're too self-critical?"

He replied, "I am, but I try not to take it personally." ✪

Reality Check

*"You must be completely awake now
and conscious on a level where
you're fully aware of the present.
That's why I like to go to Las Vegas.
There are neon signs everywhere that state,
'You must be present to win.'"*
- a Buddhist monk

Here's some advice I often impart to kids: there's right, there's wrong, and there's real. Life doesn't always fit snugly into the black-and-white concepts of right and wrong, good and bad, proper and improper. Reality comes in shades of gray. You may think your actions and opinions are correct, but they might be unwittingly wrong. What may be right for you may be unrealistic for someone else. One person's situation in life may be thoroughly removed and different from yours, yet you may judge him or her on what little knowledge you have of that person. Your reality may be wrong for another person - or for you. Many people don't face reality at all; their lives are led in quiet denial. Some people's lives are drastically changed, however, when they confront reality. Change comes from open dialogue and sharing one another's pain. Compassion comes from understanding. Understanding comes from discussion and listening.

I was in Santa Monica where two girls, both born with silver spoons in their mouths, fought one another after school. One girl came away the victor while the other was beaten and bloodied. The sister of the defeated girl sought revenge, and everyone at the school learned about it. The sister arranged another fight with the same girl.

A group of students met near the school and formed a circle around the opponents. To everyone's shock, the sister who sought revenge pulled a knife and stabbed the girl in the heart, killing her instantly.

A few of the onlookers acted swiftly to save the girl's life. However, rather than taking the victim to the nearest hospital, they unwisely drove her to an emergency room by the girl's home. She bled to death en route.

The sister then went home and overdosed on pills. The police found that the girl had taken a handful of Paxil, an anti-anxiety prescription drug.

The NBC television program *Dateline* did an entire hour-long program on the issue, and I spoke to Maria Shriver about the incident. The point I made was that some teens are so detached from reality that they don't comprehend the possible results of their actions until it's too late. We need to instill in kids the common sense to consider the consequences of what they do. ✪

An African-American girl told me about being at a 'house jam' in a garage at someone's home. Obviously, there was no parental supervision. All of the kids who were invited hung out and danced in the garage. A young DJ played music from a cheap speaker system. Suddenly, events got out of control.

"I saw it all in slow motion," the black girl told me. "One boy pushed another boy while everyone was dancing. And, you know, there's always the potential that one idiot will bring a gun to a party. Well, this was one of those nights when two idiots brought guns. Both were loaded and they both had a lot of rounds. They started shooting at each other in a small garage."

The girl got out of the harm's way quickly and was uninjured. I asked how she managed to get to safety given the suddenness and the cramped space. "Before you get to a party, you have to know the escape route."

That stunned me. I stared at her without blinking, wondering if she was serious. In fact, all of the other kids in the room nodded in agreement; they always check for exits, too. I said, "Then why go to a party where you're going to have to know how to escape?"

The illogical reply was, "Well, the police could come."

I repeated myself. "You're going to a place where you know there's danger, knowing you could die at any second...?"

The girl said, in fact, that one of the shooting victims "died in my arms. He got shot in the chest, and there was nothing I could do to stop it."

The amazing thing to me is that, despite such tragedy, kids will still go to those kinds of parties, even that African-American girl who saw the boy die in her arms. Astounded, I asked why.

"You gotta live," she said.

I argued that it isn't living if you have to deal with the fear that you might be killed. There are so many safer things to do. But the real reason that teens willingly get themselves into dangerous situations is because they want excitement. That's the draw for sixteen to eighteen-year-olds – knowing that something bad could happen. It's a sick thrill. ✪

I participated in a Police Activities League charity function that brought inner city kids to Disney World. The teens were from New York City, California, and Florida. I was among 150 police officers chaperoning about 1,000 young people. The director of activities planned a night at the Disney World discotheque, which was complete with an official Disney World DJ.

The scheduled activity was broken up early, however, because many of the kids were performing dances that were prohibited at Disney World - specifically the Tootsie Roll and the Butterfly.

For those who don't know, both the Tootsie Roll and the Butterfly are extremely lewd and suggestive. The Butterfly is performed with a chair and is similar to pole dancing that one might see in a topless nightclub.

The next day, the teens expressed their resentment. The ban at the discotheque, they felt, was unjust. After all, they were just dancing. One of the kids complained that "if the disc jockey didn't want us to dance the Tootsie Roll, then why'd he play 'Booty Call' [a hip-hop tune]? They wanted to see us dance like that."

L.B. Scott, a retired 35-year veteran police officer and a salt-of-the-earth individual, was in charge of the event. The elderly black man stood before the teens and in a stentorian voice said, "You don't understand. You kids represent the Police Activities League. Those dances are not indicative of who we are or what we stand for."

That explanation went over their heads. It suddenly became a cultural issue. "We dance like that all the time where we're from! Just because you don't do it don't mean we can't!"

Officer Scott was losing patience and control, so I intervened. I got everyone's attention. "Let me ask a question of the officers in the room. How many of you have seen a young person under the age of eighteen molested or raped?"

Every single officer raised his or her hand.

"Okay. And how many of you officers know, like I do, that in New York and Florida and California there are tens of thousands of sexual predator offenders who are not under the purview of their parole officers because they haven't registered or they've eluded authorities?"

All of the police officers' hands shot up.

"And how many of you think that there's a prime possibility that there might have been sexual predators in that disco last night just to watch young girls dance?"

All hands were raised. Some of the kids scoffed.

I was about to continue when a twenty-year-old African-American woman interrupted. Compared to most of the teens, she was dressed very conservatively; long slacks, a loose blouse, and simple shoes. She asked if she could speak, and I gave her the floor.

"Let me tell you something. I've never said this to a group before, but I feel compelled to speak up. I'm a criminal justice major from Bethune Cook College. Down here at spring break one year, I was in a T-shirt with no bra and cut-off jeans. I was drinking margaritas and having fun and partying and dancing the Tootsie Roll all day long in the hot sun. Me and my girlfriend went back up to our room, and when she left a man broke into the room. He almost raped me. And that's why I dress the way I do now."

With that, the woman took her seat. Her message came across loud and clear. ✪

In my early days at Juvenile Hall in San Francisco, I essentially listened to kids' confessions. In retrospect, I have to laugh at the absurd stories I was told, because even though there was violence involved, the sheer stupidity was both appalling and comical.

I had to counsel a young man named Jeffrey who was brought in on an assault charge. He had stabbed his own brother in the hand. "Let me tell you what happened," he said to me, as serious as a heart attack. "I come home and I see Momma putting up clothes on the line in the backyard, and my Momma's crying. I say, 'Momma, why you crying?' She told me how Shorty – that's my brother – he raped the social worker who came to our house to give us financial aid. Now I was mad, 'cause I figured she was gonna cut us off. We were gonna lose money.

"So I said, 'Where is that punk?' And I find him laughing like something's funny. So I beat his ass all over that backyard. He got mad and wouldn't let go of the fence. So to make him let go of the fence, I pulled my knife out and stabbed him right through the hand. Then I dragged him out into the house, and that pissed off my Momma 'cause we were bleeding all over her clean house. So she started to hit me in the head with a pipe. I got blood all over and Shorty got blood all over, and she chases us out onto the front porch. That's when the police showed up. And I said, 'Shit, leave us alone. This is a family disturbance.'"

You couldn't write a story like that. But that's real life for some kids – brutally absurd and pathetically comical. ✪

Here's an equally bizarre fact-is-truer-than-fiction tale from my days at Juvenile Hall. It involved two nearly identical brothers born a year apart, one of whom I'll call George. Young George was arrested and brought to see me. The charge: shooting a gas station attendant during a robbery. It occurred directly across the street from his house. I asked him to tell me what happened.

"I'm sitting there eating my Cheerios and watching Saturday morning cartoons, minding my own business. My brother comes flying through the front door and he's wearing this Hawaiian shirt. He runs up to me and says, 'Switch shirts with me.' And I said, 'For what?' Then he just punches me. So then I switched shirts with him and he runs down into the basement.

"The next thing I know, the police bust into the house and stick a sawed-off shotgun at my head. When I started to say something, the officer butt-stroked me with the gun and took me down to the jail. That's why I'm here. And they told me to shut up until I saw you because I'm not allowed to talk unless my juvenile officer is present. So here we are. Now what?"

"Wait a minute," I said. "Where's your brother now?"

George said, "He's out in the lobby with my Momma."

Skeptical, I said, "Let me see if I have this straight. Your brother shot the man at the gas station, ran across the street, switched shirts with you, hid in the basement, and now he's here at Juvenile Hall?"

"Yeah!"

I couldn't believe what I was hearing. It sounded too contrived to be true. Even so, I found the detective assigned to the case and I told him George's story.

Officers then approached the brother, who was indeed sitting in the lobby with his crying mother, and found the gun on him – the very same weapon he used in the crime! For some inexplicable reason, the idiot brought the gun with him to Juvenile Hall!

As we switched the boys over in custody, they passed by one another in the lobby. George's brother sneered at him and said, "You punk. You snitched."

Some kids are what I call NCAA - No Clue At All. ✪

A family friend called me frantically. Her seventeen-year-old son had been arrested and was sitting in a jail in Walnut Creek, California. Let's call the young man Larry. The mother begged me to pick him up and bring him home. This was a terrifying scenario for the woman; Larry was from a good home. They were an upper middle class suburban family, and they referred to their community as 'the Land That Crime Forgot.'

Larry was released on my recognizance and remanded to my custody. The other two were released to their parents' custody. As I drove him home, I asked what had happened.

Larry and two buddies devised an elaborate and preposterous scheme. Let's call the mastermind Moe and the accomplice Curly. Moe's car had been impounded at a tow service lot. His brilliant idea was to trespass on the lot, get into his own car (using his key), and rip off the stereo system from his own vehicle. Then when he paid the fine and the car was released to him, Moe could claim that the tow service had lost it and was liable to replace the radio. He could also bill his insurance company for a third stereo. That way each of them – Curly, Larry, and Moe – would have a stereo system all to himself.

I knew that the police in that community were hyper-vigilant. Many of them were ex-Special Forces, ex-Green Berets, ex-Navy Seals, etc. I wondered why the hell Larry and his knucklehead friends committed the crime there.

Their crazy plan included walkie-talkie headsets they purchased at Radio Shack and wire cutters for the chain link fence that surrounded the impound lot. They cut a hole in the fence that was six feet wide. I asked Larry why they needed such a big hole. He replied, "Why not?"

I explained that such an enormous hole was a giveaway that a burglary was being committed. To which he said, "Uh, yeah."

Larry told me he was standing at the hole, presumably as a look-out, wearing a walkie-talkie headset when a tow truck driver pulled up. The driver asked, "What are you doing?"

Larry said, "Just looking around."

"Then what happened?" I asked.

"I talked into the walkie-talkie and told my friends that I had to bolt. I said, 'I got to bolt. There's a tow truck driver here.' And I took off running as fast as I could. But by then the cops had come around the back and caught my two friends. So I ran to my step-dad's Volkswagen van and hid in there."

I said, "Your getaway car was a Volkswagen van? That's brilliant planning. Then what happened?"

"I laid on the floor of the van waiting to hear from my buddies. I kept saying into the walkie-talkie, 'Where are you guys? Where are you guys?' Then I heard these whispers. I couldn't understand them. They said, 'Pull the car around. We'll wait for you.' And I said, 'No, come to me.' So they whispered, 'Where are you?' And I had to get out of the van to look at the street sign. So then I told them what street I was on, and they said, 'We'll be right there.' Then I waited in the van and there's this rap on the door. And when I opened it up there were six cops with their guns drawn."

I kept driving and suppressed my urge to laugh. There was a long silence, and then Larry started weeping. I asked why he was crying.

He said, "They hurt me."

I asked what he meant by that. "Did they hit you, beat you, kick you?"

"No," he said sobbing. "Worse."

I pulled the car off the highway and parked on the exit. This was serious and I needed to give him my undivided attention. "Tell me what happened," I insisted.

"Okay," he said as he blubbered. "All night long, the cops kept coming down to my cell at the holdover... and turning the light on... and laughing at me."

Hilarious! I wanted to do the same thing right to the boy's face. And you know what? I see this in teenagers all the time. Too many of them simply have no common sense. ✪

I was traveling through Tijuana, Mexico, with a friend who is a professional photographer. One night, we spotted a young Caucasian teenager lying in the middle of a busy street. He was passed out drunk. Cars rolled right past him. My friend snapped photos as I raced into the street and dragged the unconscious young man to safety. Then we took him to a cheap $27 hotel room to sober up. I guessed that the college-age kid had alcohol poisoning.

The young man had no ID, no wallet, and no money, but he became coherent enough to tell me that he was a University of San Diego sophomore. He and his five friends had driven to Tijuana to party, but he somehow got separated and his friends abandoned him. He had been doing Jello shots, which, for the uninitiated, is the well-known dessert made with hard liquor. He had little memory of what had happened to him.

I drove him back to USD where he lived on campus. Then I called his parents in Coronado.

"Do you realize that your son was lying passed out in a street in Tijuana?" I told the father that I could fax him pictures as proof because my friend, a photographer, had captured the incident on film. I begged the parents, "Please, you have to talk to your son."

The boy's mother wept and asked, "What made you pull him out of the street?"

I said, "Because I have kids, too. Look, they're dopes. They're knuckleheads. That could happen to anybody's son."

Later, I learned that the young man's friends assumed that since they couldn't find him he must have taken the bus back to USD. They had no idea he had been tossed out of the bar and was lying passed out in the gutter. Kids aren't knowledgeable enough to worry, which is why episodes like that occur. ✪

I intervened for a sixteen-year-old student in a Northern California town who was dealing drugs at his high school. The boy sold $100,000 worth of drugs to sons and daughters from upper-middle class families. He was bright, good-looking, and built like a rock.

I told him, "You're going to die from this."

His deadpan response was, "I'll have lived really well until then."

It was infuriating. Fortunately, though, he had strong, loving parents to help him, and the young man eventually saw the error of his ways. Plus, he had a brush with death that turned him around.

"I had a gun shoved in my mouth, and I had to try and talk my way out of that situation. And I told myself, 'If I talk my way out of this and I'm still alive, I'm done.'"

I said, "Fear does wonderful things to you, doesn't it?"

"Yeah," he said, hanging his head. "It's not until you have the barrel of the gun in your mouth that you're thinking, 'People die like this everyday in [the drug world].' And you're thinking, 'Do I really wanna die? Isn't there anything left inside me worth caring about?'"

I asked him what he found inside himself worth caring about.

He replied, "I couldn't stand the thought of my family at the funeral saying I was a piece of shit and that it was better I was gone."

I asked how he could think that, and he told me how his father was a well-respected grocer who offered nothing but tough love.

"This isn't who I raised you to be," the boy's father said. "You make me sick. You're trading on people's pain. You're going to die. I'll come to your funeral for your mother, but I won't shed a tear."

Tough love can work. You have to be able to say to your child, 'I love you, but I hate your behavior. I'm not going to watch a train wreck in slow motion.' ✪

I was called to conduct a drug intervention in Marin County, California, the wealthiest county in the U.S.A. An athletic, sixteen-year-old son of an affluent couple was arrested with $10,000 in cash and $4,000 worth of cocaine. The son was a know-it-all; brilliant, sociopathic, and in complete denial. He insisted that he wasn't an addict, he wasn't that bad, and that everyone was blowing it all out of proportion.

I called him a liar and told him that he was sick. He wasn't just lying to me; he was lying to himself. I told him that he was infected, but not by a disease. Addiction is much more insidious.

He insisted that he was alright.

I said, "Then take a drug test."

He turned up his nose at me and smirked. "That's a violation of my rights."

The boy was a classic brat, and there was only one way to reach him. I decided to get tough. "Okay, here's something you should know," I said, jabbing my finger at his chest. "I know every judge in town, and I can get one of them to let me speak to a prosecutor about your case. Then I'll ask that prosecutor to let me testify against you. And I'm going to say on the stand that I gave you every opportunity to come clean, but you wouldn't. I'll tell them that you lied to me. You're all about denial."

The young man's face dropped in surprise. Then he sneered and mumbled, "You're so tedious."

He was a handsome kid who had it all – intelligence, material possessions, and good looks. But he was also manipulative, shrewd, and cunning. I couldn't understand why he was in such denial... until I met his parents.

We got together at a coffee shop, and I explained the gravity of the situation. I told the boy's wealthy parents that there are drug dealers who would drive to their home and kill their son over those drugs and that money.

The mother was skeptical. She arched an eyebrow. "For only $14,000?"

"Yes!"

Then the parents admitted to me that since their son stayed clean and sober for two weeks after the arrest, they rewarded him with a new Ford Tahoe.

I was outraged. "What sort of message is that, to reward a cocaine addict after only two weeks of being clean with a new SUV?"

The mother's response was, "It's not a new one! It's a 2000 model!"

There are thousands and thousands of parents in America who fear that their child won't like them. That fear causes parents to overindulge them to the point that the kids can't help but be disappointed their entire lives. By trying to fill the cavity in themselves, parents rob kids of achievement by rewarding insolence, anger, mediocrity, and addictions. ✪

Homeless children in Latin America are treated like insects, mainly because there are so many of them. As heinous and incredible as it seems, kids are sometimes abandoned and must live on the streets merely because they're the children of a former spouse. With some Latin families, when a new husband enters the fold, they force out the children from the woman's previous marriage so that they can start new families of their own. Some are abandoned as young as seven years of age. Often, their only form of survival is prostitution.

Covenant House is a Catholic organization that aids homeless children all across North America and Latin America. Their shelters for runaway children can be found in most major cities, and the work they do is extraordinary.

I was the emcee of a televised program in Denver that was produced by and exclusively for Covenant House. Bruce Harris, the head of Covenant House in Guatemala, attended that program with a young Hispanic boy. Bruce interpreted the boy's tale.

He said that his parents were killed in a septic tank explosion, so he and his brother were forced onto the streets to live. Their uncle took them in eventually, but he sold them into prostitution and forced the brothers to sell marijuana to tourists. As if that wasn't devastating enough, the boy saw his brother kicked to death by policemen in Guatemala City.

He went back to his uncle, but the man refused to let the nephew back into his house. His reasoning was that there wouldn't be enough profit with only one boy. If his brother was dead, then the boy was on his own as far as the uncle as concerned.

With no money or friends, the Latino boy starved and shivered in the cold. Then he went back to the location where his brother was murdered and lied down on the ground, waiting in abject despair for death to take him.

That was when Bruce Harris found him. Bruce took the boy to Covenant House, fed him, and nurtured him back to health. The boy said, "I knew that my mother, father, and brother prayed for me in Heaven. My life was saved so that I could meet people and tell them my story and about the work that is done at Covenant House."

When Bruce finished interpreting, I noticed a stunned silence among the other kids in attendance. Tears of pity and joy were shed for the boy. Everyone was overwhelmed with emotion. All of the North American kids instantly understood how much better their lives are in comparison.

At another taping for Covenant House in Toronto, a Mexican boy who had been homeless on the mean streets of Mexico City spoke. He said, "I'm sixteen and I was on the streets for four years. I met a girl from New York City who ran away from home because her parents wouldn't give her a telephone in her bedroom. And I was thinking, wow, forget the phone. I would just like to have parents and a roof over my head." ✪

I was in a session with a group of kids in San Francisco. I asked if anybody's anger had ever gotten so out of control that they scared themselves. Shorty, a brown-eyed 17-year-old, told me his story.

"I was always styling and never got myself in any trouble. I was up on Potrero Hill. I was walking down the street in my brand new $150 dollar Nike shoes. They should have had spotlights on me to announce my ass had arrived.

"Then this little rootie, poo-poo butt kid rolls across my brand new tennis shoes on his hot wheels bike. I said, 'Damn, kid, will you look where you're going?'

"All of a sudden his Mama comes off the porch.   A big ass S a-moan woman. She was wearing her JC Penney trailer park moo moo and that bitch had toenails like a wino's. She started kicking me in the leg. Kicking and coming and kicking and coming. Took a big chunk of meat out of my leg and I had blood pouring down on my brand new shoes. That's when I pulled out my .32 automatic. I had to have it. Everybody in my neighborhood had a .32 automatic so I carried one around, too. It was part of my style.

"I snapped a round in the chamber and I said, 'Back off, you big water buffalo bitch, before I put a whole in your ass. That's when I threw my gun down and ran home and hid on my back porch."

I asked Shorty if he still carried the gun.

"No, it scared me when I got that mad."

He agreed with me that it wasn't worth it to end up in San Quentin over a pair of tennis shoes.

Recently conducted research suggests that teenage boys can go into hormone-induced rages from testosterone that is channeled to the anger center of the brain. According to this research, they get hit with seven waves of testosterone in a day. If boys have access during these rages to weaponry, a car, a motorcycle, etc., then they may make choices that can jeopardize their lives or their futures.

Teach anger management skills to your kids. It starts with a good example. ✪

When I attended a session at a school in San Francisco, a black student, without being prompted by me or anyone else, stood up before his classmates, lifted his shirt, and said, "Look what happened to me."

He showed us four bullet-hole scars in a perfect line across his stomach. The bullets entered his body and passed straight through but, by the grace of God, never touched his vital organs. He was the victim of a drive-by shooting, and he wasn't even the intended target. The assailants merely shot everyone in sight. The boy next to him died from a shot to the chest.

I told him how sorry I was. "How did you live through it, son?"

The boy was remarkably impassive and analytical. "Man, I was really amazed at how bad it hurts when you get shot. I tried to get up after the first two [shots], but I couldn't do it. Y'know, it's not like television." ✪

I heard something similarly eerie from students at the University of California at Berkeley. A shooting took place at a party near campus, and I was called in to speak to the dazed, shaken kids in the aftermath.

For kicks, the party organizers had invited a street pimp to their house. In attendance were sons and daughters of middle-class suburban households who had no street savvy whatsoever. They thought the pimp was an intriguing novelty. "Well, he looked cool," they told me. "He was in nice clothes."

The pimp was insulted when the students laughed at him, so he shot one of the young men in the back of the head, eventually killing him. It occurred in front of the entire group at the party...yet it took a few moments before anyone realized what had happened.

"What did you think was going on?" I asked incredulously. I assumed that a gunshot and a dead body would be obvious.

"Well, the guy just kept walking around until he collapsed," one of the students said. "It's nothing like in the movies."

I told them that nothing in the movies is like real life. Nothing.

Once kids leave home, they're in the real world. And violence doesn't have a zip code. ✪

On a casual, sunny California afternoon, I took six kids, including two of my own, to a Mexican restaurant not far from my home. A disturbance erupted in the midst of our lunch, and it quickly turned violent. A short Hispanic man shattered a bottle on the edge of a table and, for reasons unknown to me, used it as a weapon. He attacked another Hispanic man by slicing him across the stomach with the jagged edges of the glass. The victim was eviscerated, but instead of waiting for medical attention he raced out of the restaurant holding his stomach with blood pouring out (I later learned why; the man was an illegal immigrant and he couldn't afford to be caught). The crazed attacker then went after a restaurant employee and cut into his arm. Fearing for the kids that were with me, I grabbed the wooden chair on which I'd been sitting and fought off the wild-eyed attacker. He ran out of the building and I chased him down the street.

A police cruiser screeched to a halt, and a husky officer with dark brown flat-top hair, dark brown eyes, and a swarthy complexion joined the chase. We caught up to the assailant and tried to get him to the ground. I said to the officer, who looked Hispanic to me, "Tell him to lay down in Spanish!"

The cop replied, "I'm Arabic."

The officer removed his collapsible steel baton and struck the Hispanic man twice, but the assailant was so high on crack that it barely fazed him. Eventually, the officer and I, each of us twice the size of the drug-addled lunatic, wrestled him to the ground and handcuffed him. Then the attacker was taken away.

News of the incident was printed on the front page of the local newspaper the next day. I was lauded for my involvement and named Marin County Peace Officer Citizen of the Year.

But a few days after the occurrence, James Pierre Louise, a Haitian-American teen who was visiting our home, said to me sarcastically, "Yo, Mr. Pritchard, I noticed you didn't use any of your conflict resolutions skills you're always talking about. You just whacked that guy in the head with a chair. Can't use no conflict resolution skills on a crack head, huh?" ✪

With a homicide investigation, you have to reconstruct when the situation between the assailant and victim fell apart. When did the confrontation become lethal?

A black teenager was crossing Cutting Boulevard in Richmond, California, which is not a safe area. The young man made eye contact with a parolee in a car and stared him down in a test of wills. It's called the hard mug, a way of communicating that 'I'm badder than you.' That led to the inevitable, "What are you looking at?"

"What are you looking at, punk?"

"I'm looking at you, bitch."

"Well, maybe you better take your sorry ass somewhere else, punk."

The senseless argument escalated until the parolee got out of the car. The black teenager was tall and muscular and ready to fight. By comparison, the parolee was a sapling that the teen could have snapped in half. But he was packing a gun.

He shot the boy sixteen times.

Later, I spoke to a group of students at John F. Kennedy High School near the scene of the crime. Of the eighteen kids I met, all eighteen of them had nightmares of being shot. Ten of the eighteen had nightmares in which they ran to the homes of their parents or grandparents where they thought they'd be safe, only to see a perpetrator kick in the door and shoot them inside the house. Those dreams showed that no place in their world was safe.

I asked the students about the senseless murder. At what point could the victim have backed out and saved his life? Yes, the perpetrator was fully to blame, but the young black man's pride got him killed, too. Kids need to know when to back out. Losing your pride isn't as sad as losing your life.

I asked, "What if you were in line at the bodega and a kid cuts in ahead of you? What are you going to do?"

A tall, heavyset Hispanic teenager answered. "Nothing. Especially if he's smaller than me. Because I know that, at my size, if he's cutting in line, he's got to be carrying a gun. So I don't say nothing. 'Cause he wants me to say something. He wants me to go off on him."

"That's a hard way to live, isn't it?" I asked.

"Yeah, but the other way is harder, where your mom is coming to your funeral." ✪

Kids I've met have an expression for when they're unaware of their surroundings. They call it sleepwalking, as in 'You can't be sleepwalking in that neighborhood.' Vigilance keeps you awake and aware of bad situations so you can get to the opposite side of the street when you sense danger. Cedric the Entertainer summed it up pretty well when he said, "When you're in the ghetto and you hear gunfire, people run away." And when you see somebody running, you join in. It's survival instinct. That's the case everywhere these days, even for suburban teens. There's no sleepwalking, especially when too many people are expressing their angers and fears with high tech weaponry. ✪

Kids aren't alone when it comes to a lack of street smarts. Adults can be equally clueless when the potential for danger is imminent.

Case in point: I was in Concord, California to give a speech at a retirement party for the police chief, and I was given a room at the Hilton Hotel. After donning a suit and tie, I exited my room and strolled through the lobby. Then I passed a young security guard who was visibly distraught, trembling and wide-eyed. I asked him if there was a problem. He pointed out to the poolside area that was thirty feet away outside the lobby.

There sat fifteen to twenty hardcore gangbangers partying by the pool. I could tell in five seconds that they were all parolees because of the scars and prison tattoos they displayed, specifically the teardrops on their faces. Convicts tattoo one teardrop on their cheeks for every year spent in prison. Some of the men had dead eyes, so I knew that those guys and their rough women were not to be messed with. But that wasn't the real cause for concern.

A middle-aged suburban housewife stood with arms akimbo berating the gang members about their "foul language." Her two young children sat across the pool on lounge chairs, and she didn't want her kids to hear their cursing. She looked like Mrs. Republican Party, and her demeanor was that of a schoolmarm with naughty boys and girls. She had no idea what possible jeopardy she was in.

"You know what?" the woman said sternly. "My children do not need to hear your cursing."

The gang members chuckled, and one of them said, "Yeah? Well, fuck you and your children, okay?"

The young security guard beside me mumbled, "Oh, God, lady. Just shut up, shut up. I need back up so bad." We were too far away for either the mother or the parolees to hear him.

Then I heard the woman say, "You people are reprehensible."

That evoked wild laughter from the gangbangers. "Reprehensible! Hey, did you hear that? We're all reprehensible. Hey, man, did you know you're reprehensible? Yeah, you're reprehensible. Maybe we should call ourselves the Reprehensibles!" Then they started singing. "We're the Reprehensibles, yeah, the Reprehensibles…"

The woman was aghast. "Who do you think you are? I don't know how you think you can get away with this behavior. Do you know where you are? This is a Hilton."

The parolees exploded with laughter at that comment. I felt like walking up to the woman and telling her politely to grab her children, pack up her poolside belongings, and go to her room. Mrs. Republican Party was so out of touch that she must have thought she was at the country club yelling at some insolent brats who were behaving inappropriately. She didn't realize that she was facing down dangerous young men, most of them between 20 to 30 years of age, who would kill her on the spot and not think twice about it.

With the security guard freaking out, I decided to take action. I approached the woman, who was still scolding the gangbangers, and as calmly as I could I said, "Ma'am, please don't talk anymore." She was immediately obedient. No doubt the sight of a big white man in a suit and tie intimidated her, which was surely not the case for the parolees. I scanned the gang for the one man who was the most sober and least involved. I spotted him and casually approached.

"Here's the deal," I said. "You've got security scared, you've got this woman scared, and I'm scared. So here's what we need to do. Local police are on the way. That's the bottom line. Now, I know that you guys probably have stuff up in your rooms that you probably don't need up there. You need to get that stuff out of there right now, because if there are guns or dope or anything up there, the cops are going to book you for it. So I suggest that you calmly and quickly and quietly get going. I've been a parole agent long enough to know that you have maybe three minutes at best to clear everything out."

That was all it took. There was no hassle. None of the gangbangers said a word. They calmly got up and left for their rooms. Shortly after that, they departed from the Hilton.

Mrs. Republican Party still had no concept of the potential violence that was narrowly avoided. She watched the parolees saunter away, and in a vinegary tone she said, "They are so lucky."

Not since George Armstrong Custer became the butt of the joke when he said "Surround them, men!" has anyone proved so foolish. Sometimes an Ivy League education is no substitute for being streetwise. ✪

A young gangbanger once told me, "I didn't shoot that guy 'cause I wanted to. I shot him 'cause I had to. There was peer pressure from my gang. They just looked at me and said, 'C'mon, man, you gotta shoot him now.' So I did."

This is the world kids live in today. Whether it's in a suburban California high school or in the Bronx or in Tallahassee, students tell me they feel that they have to be 'strapped.' They believe that having a gun is a necessity. The mentality is, 'If they've got a gun, I've got to have a gun.' It's a false sense of strength.

A student I met in San Rafael, California, said it best: "Too many boys in America are crying with bullets instead of tears." ✪

Violence isn't solely a male dilemma, of course. I spoke to an assembly at a New Jersey school for a couple of hours about violence and peace. Then I surprised the kids by addressing the flip side of the issue.

"If there was a fight between two senior girls," I asked, "how many of you would watch that fight, even if it was between two really attractive girls who were both popular and friendly?"

Nearly every kid raised his or her hand...even after I'd spent an afternoon with them discussing violence prevention. I had to laugh derisively; clearly, my message didn't get through.

"Okay," I continued. "Now that you're there to watch the girls fight, is it more likely or less likely that they'll attack one another?"

The kids knew that it was more likely.

"Then what are you going to do?" I asked.

The reply was, "Saying 'Ooooo!' gets a fight started faster than anything." As in, "Oooooo! You gonna let her say that about you? Ooooooo!"

I said, "Okay, so then the girls start fighting. They grab each other by the hair. Now what do you do?"

The kids replied, "We encourage them. We say, 'Fight, fight, fight.'"

"Now the crowd is cheering and hooting. The girls are punching and pulling. They're scratching and tearing each other's clothes. Then, one girl throws down her opponent...and she lands on a pipe...which goes through her body...right through her spleen...The pipe is sticking out and blood is spurting everywhere...She can't move...and it's going to take a long time for the ambulance to come...The girl left standing freaks out because she sees what she's done to the girl she was fighting...What happens to all of you watching the fight? You all bounce, running away from the scene. But you were the people encouraging the violence. It takes the ambulance six minutes to get there – that's on a good day. The girl has lost eleven units of blood. She's near death. Her mother, a licensed practical nurse, and her father, a fireman who has spent his entire life working to rescue people, are in the hospital praying for their daughter's life. They're in jeopardy of losing someone they love because of the violence that you encouraged because you found it amusing."

I stopped speaking momentarily and looked at the unblinking eyes and heads that were hanging in shame. Then I continued. "Can this happen? Does it happen? Of course it does. Everyday. I'm going to leave you now. I just hope that some of you realize that your relationship to violence is sad." ✪

In February 2001, freshman David Edward Attias, 18, ran over five of his classmates at the University of California at Santa Barbara. Four were killed. The fifth victim, a young man who lived in my neighborhood, was critically injured but survived. Attias reportedly drove his car up to sixty miles per hour through a residential area, struck nine vehicles, and then hit the pedestrians. He then got out of the car and shouted, "I am the angel of death." Pictures from his trial show him as a slightly older version of the beloved Harry Potter, innocuous and baby-faced. Yet the young man was suffering from delusions that some say were brought on by drugs. He was later convicted on four counts of murder.

When I spoke to students from UCSB about the matter, I was appalled by what they told me. Every kid in the dorm where Attias lived, according to those I spoke to, knew that the strange young man was routinely "flipping out" and that he was "cranked out of his mind." (Crank is methamphetamine.)

"Then why didn't you tell an adult?" I asked with veins nearly popping out of my head from anger. "Why didn't you get help? Why didn't you get someone to intervene?"

The mumbled response I got was, "Well, we were just freshmen. We didn't want to get him in trouble or anything."

"Well, now there are four dead kids!" I said in exasperation.

Every one of the students in that dorm were deemed highly intelligent by virtue of the fact that they were attending UCSB, a state school where it's difficult to get accepted. Most of them graduated high school with 4.2 grade point averages. Yet none of them even considered seeking a mental health professional. None of them had the common sense to get involved before Attias got hurt or injured someone else.

There's an expression: Tell me, and I'll forget. Show me, and I'll remember. Involve me, and I'll understand. Peer counseling, which teaches kids to reach out to disgruntled, angry, or isolated individuals, benefits the youths and the community. The earlier we teach this to our kids, the safer they'll become. ✪

Occasionally, I ask students at school assemblies how many of them play point-and-shoot video games. The responses are loud and enthusiastic.

"How many of you guys play Grand Theft Auto?" They cheer. Boys are all too familiar with that violent game. I sucker them in with more questions.

"You get to run over homeless people, right?" More cheers.

"And you get to beat prostitutes with a tire iron, right?" They scream with gleeful recognition.

"And then you can shoot policemen and paramedics, right?" Even more roars.

Then I tell them that the man who created the game Doom once admitted that he was "a deeply disturbed person, and your children are walking around inside my mind, but they made me a millionaire."

Then I point out that the killers at Columbine High School were hooked on Doom. The disturbed young man in West Paducah, Kentucky who shot his classmates had never fired a weapon before. Even so, he had an eight-round clip and he hit eight students directly in the head. Video games helped him become an expert marksman. SWAT teams all across America have been trained to use just two words to get kids to put down their weapons, and it has been unusually effective. Those words are: Game over. That's all it takes, and the young perpetrators obey. Then I tell the students how many of the victims of school shootings were amazed to discover how truly painful it is to get shot. Kids are so desensitized by video game violence that they don't comprehend reality.

Whenever I explain these realities to school assemblies, those roars of glee are quickly replaced with pensive silence. That's when I drive home my point. In a voice dripping with righteous, regal earnestness like a bad Shakespearean actor, I say, "But those things won't happen to me. Oh, no, not me. I am immortal. I shall live forever. I'm a teenager! Nothing bad can happen to me. I have good parents who love me very much. I will be able to live out my life to the end. I will be able to choose exactly when and where I wish to die. Because I am a teenager!"

And then, to emphasize my point, I walk off the stage. ✪

What You Do When Nobody's Looking

Recommend to your children virtue;
that alone can make them happy, not gold.
Ludwig van Beethoven

Here's my recurring message to kids: Character is defined by what you do when nobody's looking.

I knew a girl in St. Louis who became pregnant at the age of seventeen. Let's call her Cheryl. She made a mess of her life, but she shifted blame to anyone and everyone else. The pregnancy, she claimed, was due to molestation; it was the boy's fault. Then when that excuse didn't wash, she blamed her devoutly Catholic parents for not providing her enough information about sex. When the baby arrived, she passed it off on everyone she could – her parents, her siblings, her friends, her relatives - and wouldn't mother the child herself. Meanwhile, Cheryl ran off to lead a life of desperation and wild abandon with alcohol and drugs.

I confronted her. I wondered how she had gotten into such a sad situation, because I knew that she came from a good family. I told her that her infant was a gift. That baby was brought into her life to make Cheryl realize some hard truths.

For whatever reasons, Cheryl took my advice to heart. She cleaned up and entered nursing school. She later became a skilled ER nurse. Her life changed completely. Today, Cheryl's daughter works with her in the emergency room as a nurse. Their purposes in life were to teach each other. Cheryl had to learn the hard way, but her daughter was spared that hardship.

If you can take the bad things in life and cope with them, then you owe it to others to teach what you've learned. ✪

I met a praiseworthy young African-American man who attended Lincoln High School in San Francisco. He lived in the disreputable Hunter's Point district.

He told a group of fellow students, "Hey, man, teachers here just don't get it. They judge you without knowing what your world is like. They don't know what you have to do to live.

"Last week I was on my way to school. I get bused in here from across town, so I'm standing there waiting for the bus. And there was this baby wandering around in the cold with nothing on but a diaper. I freaked out. Who was in charge of this baby? I had to pick up the baby and wrap her in my jacket. There was nobody around to give her to, so I missed my bus. It was ten minutes before I found an adult who knew the little girl. There was a lady who took the baby from me to give to its mother.

"I got on the next bus and I was sulking and I was thinking to myself, 'Why do I have to live in a neighborhood where people don't know how to take care of babies?'

"When I got to school, I was three minutes late and I had to report to the office. The admissions lady got in my face and hollered at me for being tardy. All the pain and sorrow had gotten to me and I just started going off on her.

"I said, 'You don't know what I had to do to get here today! You don't know anything about my life! So don't judge me!'

"And you know what? I got suspended for two days. I tried to tell them what was going on, but they just didn't get it. They said I was disrespectful. Maybe I was but so were they. The problem was that nobody was taking time to understand."

Every person needs the validation of understanding. If we refuse to take time to hear the whole story, we miss the point of being parents or educators. ✪

Andy was a muscular teenager, tough and broad-shouldered. His father, the hub of the wheel around which the family revolved, was a well-respected San Mateo, California firefighter. Tragically, he suffered a fatal heart attack right in front of his son. Andy's family, especially his mother, was overcome with grief.

After his father's passing, Andy helped his family make ends meet. He took on a job working forty hours a week at an auto body shop. He also attended high school full time.

Andy was among a group of students I met during a session at his San Mateo high school. I asked the kids if anyone had gotten so angry that they lost control of themselves.

Andy replied: "This kid shows up at school antagonizing and insulting my friends who are girls. This kid graduated already with no life and kept coming back to high school. There was a confrontation, words were exchanged, and I body slammed him into a car. Then I started to choke him. He was a few seconds from death when I remembered who my father raised me to be and my mother needed me to be. I let go. I got in my truck and drove to a lake. I cried for two hours because it scared me that I could end somebody's life just like that."

Grief that's not addressed can turn to anger, anger to rage, rage to violence. Getting between a kid's grief and anger can cushion the next choice from being so desperate. ✪

Cynicism is common in kids and perhaps the worst character trait of all. In some kids, however, it's so pervasive that they're completely emotionally detached. They have no interest at all in the bigger picture of life. I was in Los Angeles meeting with over 200 high school students, and I was struck by how unengaged and unconcerned they seemed towards the world around them.

"How many of you here," I asked, "have your own hot tub at home?"

Every hand was raised.

"And how many of you have your own family swimming pool?"

Every hand went up.

"How many of you have your own car, or will have your own car when you're sixteen?"

All hands went up.

"So then it's pretty difficult for you guys to worry about life beyond yourselves, isn't it? Your comfort levels are so high that you're not really engaged in global issues. Right?"

A stylishly dressed girl with perfect brunette hair raised her hand. She spoke up without any forethought. "Okay, like, it's really hard for me to get into worrying about whether people in Nicaragua have big screen TVs."

That nonsensical comment hit me in such a wave that I collapsed into a chair, not only because it saddened me that a group of kids could be so disconnected from bigger realities beyond their own lives but because that girl felt that it was acceptable to say what she said. In some kids, lack of caring about others is too typical, and that's pitiful. ✪

The gap between the haves and the have-nots is quite distinct in some schools. Kids that come from well-to-do families don't always understand how some of their complaints might seem ludicrous to others. That was true when I visited Aptos, California. Some students were the children of upper class business executives. Others were the sons and daughters of poverty-level field workers. The latter were often Hispanic. The kids were discussing their various problems when, out of nowhere, a skinny little girl told us this tale of woe.

"Oh my God, my father promised me a new BMW convertible for my sixteenth birthday, right? So I had my girlfriends over to celebrate my birthday. We were just hanging. And my father said, 'Look outside the window.' So I looked outside, right? And there in the driveway was a Chevy Malibu convertible all tied up with a ribbon. I just burst into tears and ran to my room, 'cause I was so hurt that it wasn't what he promised me. And then my Dad backed that car out, right? And he pulled in the BMW that I asked for. He only bought the Malibu as a joke to fool me."

There was a long pause.

I had been keeping eye contact with one of the Hispanic boys, a hip kid who looked like he could have been a band member of Los Lobos. He had a sense of humor about life, which instantly made him my kindred spirit. He said little during the entire session, but when he did speak it made me howl with laughter.

He looked at me and said, "Hey, excuse me, can you ask her if my Mom and Dad can have the joke?" ✪

Sometimes, I gather groups of impoverished immigrant school-children and show them copies of the Robb Report. Ostensibly, it's a magazine, but in reality it's more like a catalogue marketed towards the super, super wealthy. Page after page shows extravagant items for sale that the average person simply could never afford; yachts, outrageously expensive jeweled wristwatches, pens costing $1,000, lavish wonders with nearly obscene price tags. I show it to Afghani kids, Vietnamese kids, Cambodian kids, and other children from traditionally underprivileged corners of the world.

Each time, I see the same three reactions. First, they will say, "Wow." The opulence astonishes them. The second reaction is, "Who gets this magazine?" I tell them that it's sent to billionaires. The third reaction is, "This isn't fair." It strikes them as unjust for people to have such luxury while others don't even have enough food.

When we encourage children to strive towards external validations, the ultimate end is summed up in that tongue-in-cheek expression, 'He who dies with the most toys, wins.' Kids with strong spirits understand how wrong that is. ✪

I spoke to students at one of America's finest universities, and an arrogant young man asked me about my background. "So you were a medic in Viet Nam and you've helped people on the streets. Right?"

He asked the question as if he were an attorney who didn't believe my alibi. I told him he was correct.

He said, "My father thinks that people like you have a personality flaw."

The tactless statement stunned me, but I replied, "It seems to me that your father may be one of those people who never helped build America yet lives off it."

The young man looked down his nose at me and said, "Well, I'll tell my Dad you said that."

Later, an Asian-American student approached me. "I am so sorry that guy said that to you. When I hear guys like him say those kinds of things, man, I get sad. I'm just glad we have a middle class, because I think the poor people would have killed us all by now." ✪

Selena had a beautiful round Latino face that held a smile as wide as her entire five-foot-tall frame. Occasionally, I meet soft-spoken, lovely souls like Selena who have already figured out life; they're just sitting back to enjoy it. Selena was the first of her family born in America, yet she spoke only Spanish at home. She was blessed with parents who loved her.

In one of my sessions, I asked, "Have you ever seen anyone who was isolated or alone?"

Selena answered. "I have this girl in my PE class. She's kind of big, you know. I hear the kids call her names in the hall. One day, these popular girls asked this big girl to be in their group for exercises. But they only did it to make fun of her. They would stand behind her and imitate her trying to touch her toes. I wanted to talk to her that day but my friends said, 'If you talk to her, then you'll get picked on, too.'

"We were having this group discussion in PE class about friendship, and the teacher said that when we get down we need to talk to our friends. And the big girl said, 'I don't have any friends.'

"I felt so bad. I started to think that there were 900 kids in this school and not one of us had made her a friend. The next day, we were supposed to get partners for this tennis thing. I asked her if she wanted to be my partner, and she said no. The next day, I asked her again, and she said okay."

I asked Selena what made her approach that girl again, even though she said no the first time.

"I guess I figured she was hurt by everyone and didn't trust nobody. I was just going to keep trying till she trusted me and knew I wasn't going to hurt her. Now she's my friend. She's big and I'm small, so I feel safe knowing she would back me up if anybody messed with little me."

"What did you personally learn from this, Selena?"

"That one person gets everything started, but you have to take that first step." ✪

Sandy McDonnell of the McDonnell Douglas Corporation wanted to find a way to help build character in kids. He knows that children need internal assets like courage and compassion in order to succeed. So he organized a series of character education forums in which orators traveled the country speaking to educators who could then pass along character-building skills to their pupils. The group of speakers included me and actor Tom Selleck, among others. Approximately 500 teachers and 50 students attended each forum. I hosted the question and answer symposiums with the kids who were selected because they were class leaders in their schools. The purpose was to show the educators how I interacted with students and why I was successful at it.

At the symposium held in St. Louis, I asked the kids, "If you knew you could get away with it, how many of you would cheat on SATs to get higher grades so you could get into the right school?"

Every single hand was raised.

After I thanked the students for their honesty, a sophomore student from Lima, Missouri raised her hand. I recognized her and she said, "My Mom and Dad home schooled me, and I was just wondering... I don't know, maybe this the wrong question, but... When did grades become more important than learning?" ✪

I met a boy with a face like a Picasso painting. We'll call him William. He was a pudgy third grader. William was so badly disfigured that his left eye was several inches higher than his right eye and his nose was slightly off center. I assumed that the person with him was his full-time aide.

I asked the third-grade class if anyone wanted to speak up about what it was like to be picked on. When William came to the front of the class, I assumed he would talk about his personal experiences with teasing and name-calling. It seemed obvious that he would be the brunt of cruel jokes. But I was surprised by what he said.

"You are all nice to me because I'm so different, and you do not hurt me. But you hurt my friend Owen's heart. Owen was the first person from kindergarten who was my friend. And when you hurt Owen's heart, you hurt my heart. Because he is my friend. So please don't hurt Owen anymore."

Every adult in the classroom was weeping, including me. When you see a child like William who thinks outside of himself, you know that the parents have raised a child that lives his life from his heart. ✪

Afterword

I'm a blessed and fortunate individual to travel the country and speak to youth about making good choices in their lives. But parents mustn't wait for someone like me to offer guidance to kids. We adults must set the example for our own children.

How? Open up communication with your kids. Listen, don't talk. Ask for their opinions. Ask how they're feeling. Too many of us in today's society read and listen to adult experts on what youth are thinking when their young faces are staring right at us.

And parents must have a sense of humor. When my young son came home ashamed of a poor test grade, I told him I was going to go get Arnold Schwarzenegger and we were going back to school and march into that teacher's room and arm wrestle her! He chuckled and then we sat and talked about ways we could work together on the problem. Encourage a sense of humor and help develop it in them. When you gather for dinner, let them have their moment, imitating teachers and reenacting scenes from the day. Humor is a powerful tool, a proven healer, a great common denominator, and it can save you from the darkest moments.

During my days working at Juvenile Hall, I met a young guy who was arrested for grand theft. Julio was a solid kid from a highly regarded family and just got caught up with the wrong crowd. I always knew that if I could get a kid to laugh at himself or with me then I could make a connection. After an hour of trying my darnedest to reach Julio, however, he suddenly stood up at yelled, "I'm tired of everybody telling me what to do! I'm gong to join the Marine Corps!"

I busted out laughing and said, "Oh, yeah, nobody *there* will tell you what to do!"

Julio laughed at what he said and we sat down and worked things out. Humor works wonders.

It's also important to get kids involved in their community. Do hands-on volunteer work together. Expose them to the less privileged. That can build character. I've watched my own children benefit tremendously by assisting people in need.

Teach them by your example not to be afraid of those that are different. Break through cynicism and fear and bring compassionate involvement into the world.

But the most vital and constructive thing parents can do is listen. Put aside judgments. Be open-minded. Be patient. And persevere.

Listening shows love. Love to listen.

About Michael Pritchard

Michael travels throughout North America speaking to youths, administrators, and parents helping them to gain insight into themselves and the choices kids make. He speaks to students of all ranges – elementary school, middle school, high school, and college – on issues of resolving conflicts, giving and attaining respect, dealing with anger, and preventing violence. In his presentations, Mike uses his gift of comedy to gain attention. He reenacts real life stories that exemplify the issues that need to be addressed. Most importantly, he teaches kids how to make positive changes in their lives.

After a typical school assembly, Michael gathers small discussion groups in which he talks directly with the students. He gives them hypothetical situations that force them to make difficult decisions. The results help kids examine how their choices might affect others. He then guides them through self-discovery to make the right choices. Often, these intimate discussions launch admissions of children's stored pain. Watching kids hear each other's pain is a stunningly effective tool that Michael has used countless times to help alter young lives for the better.

Aside from speaking to youth groups and schools, Michael Pritchard has also addressed national political leaders, law enforcement agents, public service groups, and a variety of business leaders. Everyone learns from the tales he tells of youth across America and the results of positive change in their lives.

Michael is most noted, however, for the six PBS television educational series that follow his formula for interacting with youth.

They include: *The Power of Choice, You Can Choose, Big Changes, Big Choices, Peacetalks,* and *SOS: Saving Our Schools.* Each series shows him addressing an assembly and interacting in small groups on a variety of subjects guiding them to make good choices.

Michael has received the President's Volunteer Action Award, the Guardsman of the Year Award, a commendation from the Office of the Attorney General, the Josephine Duveneck Humanitarian Award, the prestigious Marin Community Foundations' Beryl Buck Award for achievement in promoting non-violence, and numerous other honors. He is a member of the Board of Directors for the Special Olympics, Ronald McDonald House, and the California Association of Peer Programs, among other organizations. Michael was the Master of Ceremonies for Pope John Paul II's visit to San Francisco. He has been profiled in *Time* magazine, the *Christian Science Monitor*, the *San Francisco Chronicle*, and many other publications. He has been seen on CNN, the Today Show, and CBS' Sunday Morning with Charles Kuralt. Michael was awarded a Doctorate of Humane Letters for a lifetime of work inspiring, motivating and profoundly touching the minds and hearts of thousands of children and people across the country. He and his wife and three children live in Northern California.

MICHAEL PRITCHARD RESOURCES

Videotapes available include:

LIFESTEPS

THE POWER OF CHOICE

SAVING OUR SCHOOLS

YOU CAN CHOOSE!

BIG CHANGES, BIG CHOICES

PEACETALKS

For more information, please visit

www.michaelpritchard.com

Printed in the United States
102551LV00011B/1-75/A